The Plain Man's Guide to Wine

ERRATUM

The publisher regrets that a small
illustration is missing from page 33.
A line drawing, similar to that on
page 29, should appear on this page.

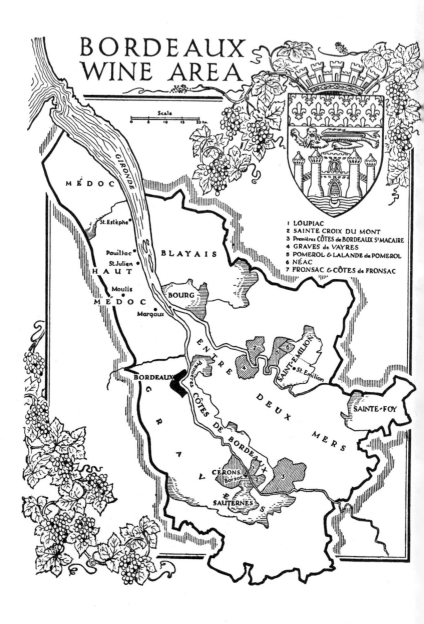

BORDEAUX WINE AREA

Scale

MÉDOC

St.Estèphe

Pauillac

St.Julien

HAUT

MÉDOC

Moulis

Margaux

GIRONDE

BLAYAIS

BOURG

ENTRE

DEUX

MERS

SAINTE-FOY

BORDEAUX

G R A V E S

Premières CÔTES DE BORDEAUX

CÉRONS

SAUTERNES

SAINT-EMILION

St.Emilion

1 LOUPIAC
2 SAINTE CROIX DU MONT
3 Premières CÔTES de BORDEAUX St MACAIRE
4 GRAVES de VAYRES
5 POMEROL & LALANDE de POMEROL
6 NÉAC
7 FRONSAC & CÔTES de FRONSAC

The
Plain Man's Guide
To Wine

RAYMOND POSTGATE
REVISED BY JOHN ARLOTT

London
MICHAEL JOSEPH

First published in Great Britain by
MICHAEL JOSEPH LTD
52 *Bedford Square*
*London, W.C.*1
SEPTEMBER 1951
SECOND IMPRESSION FEBRUARY 1952
THIRD IMPRESSION (REVISED) JUNE 1953
FOURTH IMPRESSION NOVEMBER 1954
FIFTH IMPRESSION (REVISED) NOVEMBER 1955
SIXTH IMPRESSION (REVISED) MAY 1957
SEVENTH IMPRESSION (REVISED) JANUARY 1959
EIGHTH IMPRESSION (REVISED) JANUARY 1960
NINTH IMPRESSION (REVISED) JULY 1960
TENTH IMPRESSION (REVISED) APRIL 1962
ELEVENTH IMPRESSION (REVISED) DECEMBER 1963

*

NEW EDITION, RESET, REVISED AND
ENLARGED, SEPTEMBER 1965
SECOND IMPRESSION NOVEMBER 1965
THIRD IMPRESSION (REVISED) FEBRUARY 1967
SIXTEENTH IMPRESSION (REVISED AND RESET) SEPTEMBER 1976

© 1951–76 *by Raymond Postgate*

ISBN 0 7181 0824 8

*Set and printed in Great Britain by Hollen Street Press Ltd
at Slough and bound by James Burn at Esher*

Mihi est propositum
In taberna mori;
Vinum sit appositum
Morientis ori,

Vt dicant cum venerint
Angelorum chori:
'Deus sit propitius
Huic potatori.'

CANON WALTER MAP

It is my proposed aim to die in an inn; let wine be placed to the lips of the dying man, so that, when they come, the choruses of angels may say: 'God be kind to this drinker.'

The translation does not do justice to the Latin of this agreeable poem. *Propositum*, for example, has an intentionally formal character: 'this is the proposition,' it says, as if the matter were put before a meeting and the Canon were looking round for a seconder. Nor are there any false quantities; carpers have objected that *mori* appears to rhyme with *ōri* but it does not, it rhymes with *chori*, which also has a short O. Observe too, how, being a Prebendary of St Paul's and Chaplain to Henry II as well as a Canon, the author writes *chori*, choruses; for you or me, perhaps, one brisk cherub will suffice, but as an escort to heaven he knows he is entitled to at least two ranks of angels.

R.P.

PREFACE

The Plain Man's Guide to Wine is one of several memorials to an interesting and outstanding man. Raymond Postgate was a radical, a classical scholar, a social historian and a practising journalist; an idealist of unquestionable integrity with a quick, questing mind, a sense of humour and of justice, and an informed taste in wine and food.

When he died, in 1971, he left his *History of the British People* (written with G. D. H. Cole), *Revolution from 1789 to 1906*; perceptive biographies of John Wilkes, Robert Emmet and his father-in-law, George Lansbury; translations of *Pervigilium Veneris* and *The Agamemnon of Aeschylus*; half a dozen novels, and a revision of H. G. Wells's *Outline of History* as mark of his scholarly and literary quality.

In another aspect of his life, he founded the Good Food Club and its *Guide* and, with his unpaid aides, sustained both through their precarious early years. He published the first edition of *The Plain Man's Guide to Wine* in 1951; and revised it for the last time for the seventeenth impression in 1967; it undoubtedly helped many from hesitancy into pleasurable wine-drinking. Because Raymond Postgate's mind and motives were clear, his basic approach remains completely right. He intended his book as 'a plain guide for the would-be drinker who comes fresh to the subject, not a reference book for the expert'. This edition is meant simply to continue his purpose.

He noted in his last edition that 'through devoted attention to duty, I am now able to say that every one (not merely most) of the verdicts on wines or firms are the result of my own experience'. In the decade since that last revision, however, the technology of vinification has developed rapidly and radically – he might wonder whether entirely for the best; wine legislation has been fundamentally reshaped; and whole national attitudes towards wine-making have altered. If he had experienced this transformation, his essential clear-mindedness would certainly have led him to change some former judgements; and alter his advice accordingly. Those adjustments have been made.

It was an immense compliment to one who held him in affectionate admiration, and learnt much about wine from him, when the invitation to revise this *Guide* was proffered jointly by his sons and his publishers. The intent has been to maintain it – with all the pride he had in it – as Raymond Postgate's book.

J.A.

CONTENTS

For Quick Reference

1. The Elements

Simplicity of wine-drinking – Falsehoods of the Wine Snob – 'Drink what you like' – Smoking – List of chief varieties of wine – Apéritifs, table wines, dessert wines – Temperature of wine, shaking of wine, wine with food – The vintages that matter – Glasses – How to taste wine – The minimum of knowledge on a postcard.

WINE DRINKING is easy. That it is pleasant everyone who can read the Bible or English literature at all knows very well. That it is health-giving in moderation (and nothing is good in immoderation) has been re-stated so frequently that only the most obstinate deny it. But there is a wide belief that to drink wine wisely and with profit is a difficult thing. There are many men and women today who would like to drink wine with their meals, and even more to offer a friend or a business acquaintance a glass of wine, but who fear that they will make some grave mistake when they try to do so. They think that there exists a great body of knowledge about wine which is hidden from them, and without which they will perhaps be robbed, probably look silly and certainly not enjoy themselves.

This fear is baseless, and the object of this first chapter is to dispel it. A very small amount of knowledge, so small that a meticulous man could write it on a card and keep it in his pocket, is enough to enable one to order wine confidently in a restaurant, to defy all but the most highly paid of wine waiters, and to offer guests in one's home a reasonable dinner with wine of the right kind, served so that both you and they will enjoy it. Little more learning is enough to accumulate an unpretentious cellar and enjoy conversation about wine-drinking, which is among the most soothing of minor pleasures.

The first kind of knowledge will be offered to the reader in this first chapter. Since the early editions of this book one major problem has been solved for him by the laws of the Common Market. If a wine merchant or shipper cannot – or will not – print on the label of every bottle, under the official warranty of its country of origin, exactly where a wine was made, he can give it only a brand name. Why is there this uneasiness about wine drinking? For two reasons, I think, the first a break of continuity in all English-speaking countries. Until the present century was well advanced, many young men, and fewer young women, learnt from the example of their parents and their own experiments how to drink wine. They might decide that they preferred beer – and why not? They might discover that they belonged to the unfortunate minority who should never drink at all, just as there are some who should never drive a car. But mostly they would settle down into an easy and natural habit of living as before them did their grandfathers and great-grandfathers and great-great-grandfathers and so on far beyond the Middle Ages. But the present generation has not been allowed to carry on the tradition; it has not the *instinct* of wine drinking which comes from having been accustomed to wine in youth. It has to relearn a natural habit. This cannot be done from books. Books will help; but appreciation of wine can only be learnt by the drinking of wine.

The second reason is that there is an especial nuisance in the wine world, which is to it as the green fly is to the rose, the black fly to the broad bean and the saw-fly to the apple. This local pest flourishes upon the uncertain and diffident, of whom there are many just now, and frightens them away from wine. He is called a Wine Snob. He is to be found in a large number of bars and hotels and in certain clubs, but he exuberates most and does most harm in suburban homes.

A Wine Snob is a man (the vice is much more masculine than feminine) who uses a knowledge of wine, often imperfect, to impress others with a sense of his superiority. He may have a foundation of kindliness and good sense – since he drinks wine it is probable that he has – but he has built on it a palace of conceit. He enjoys not the wine, but a series of elaborate conventions. Most of these have no adequate reason behind them, but he is able to suggest that ignorance of them is socially disastrous. He never positively says this; he insinuates it by telling anecdotes of others who made errors which he was able to correct. You must recognize the five or seven different kinds of glasses in which various wines should be served, he suggests. He indicates that you must know the good, the moderate and the bad years since 1900 for seven different categories of wine. (Theoretically this would involve memorizing just over 1,300 items.) You should be able to distinguish not only between claret and burgundy, but between various châteaux in the Bordeaux area; you must know at what temperatures to serve each wine and exactly what food to take with it; you must follow a fixed order of wines in serving; he also conveys that there are many essential refinements connected with decanting and cork-drawing. If in company you cannot meet any of these tests you have failed socially. The young woman you are taking out to dinner will be humiliated, the business friend will dine next time with your rival, you will give your wife stomach-ache, the waiter will sneer – in short, you will make an exhibition of yourself.

The Wine Snob does not say, in so many words: 'You'd better stick to beer,' because that would destroy his real object. What he wants is that he should continue to be envied; 'for ever should you love and he be fair.' But in fact he drives the inexperienced man who would like to drink wine back to bottled beer and blended whisky. Just as the black fly by destroying the broad bean kills its own sustenance, so he destroys what he feeds on and needs – an audience. It shall be shown that what he says is 50 per cent. unnecessary and nearly 50 per cent. untrue.

The first rule for a wine drinker is: 'Drink what you like.' The motto of Rabelais' Abbey was *Fay ce que vouldras* – Do what you wish; that is the motto of every sensible wine drinker. Don't pretend. Most, but not all experienced wine drinkers prefer 'dry' wines; all Wine Snobs say they do. But if you prefer sweet wines, say so, and drink them. For two good reasons – the first, that you will not be able to keep the pretence up indefinitely, and will be found ignobly drinking Rich Ruby Wine of Port Character in the Private Bar; the second that, as mostly happens when you tell lies about matters of importance, you are probably injuring yourself. You probably *should* prefer sweet wines to begin with, because you probably need them. In nearly all countries sugar was rationed during the war – in Great Britain it still was rationed as late as 1953 – and many people still have a residuary hankering for it. It is much better taken in the form of a good Sauternes than in chocolates, sweets or candy, which damage the teeth, or in ice-cream which strains the stomach. In any case, young and growing human beings need more sugar, and up to about twenty-two a taste for sweeter wines is natural. Finally, women are said always to have an inclination to rather sweeter wines. Why, I do not know; but it is risky to go against natural instincts, and it is probable that most of the girls in the country would be the better for a half-bottle of Graves with their meals. If therefore people around you are praising dry wines, you can with complete confidence announce a preference for a full, round port. (You will have important supporters among the senior members of the Cavalry Club, anyhow.) What is true, however, is that as time goes on it is probable (not certain) that your taste for sweet wines will diminish. Partly, this will be merely because your initial demand for sugar has been satisfied. Your first delight in madeiras, malagas, ports, sweet sherries, and sauternes is the simple and innocent greed of a child let loose in a sweet shop. Midway through his second pound of chocolate creams doubts will overcome him; so they will you. But in larger part it will be a definite development in taste, an enlargement of your capacity for pleasure. It is comparable to the change that takes place in the lover of music or of poetry. He begins, usually, by thinking in adolescence that the *Londonderry Air* is the most lovely thing possible in music and Swinburne or Ella Wheeler Willcox the most inspiring of poets. Only later and slowly does he learn to like Beethoven or T. S. Eliot. Some never go so far; some never leave the starting-post. They are not for that bad citizens. But it is probable that you who read this will find before long, that (say) a middle-aged noble claret, served gently and drunk slowly, provides you a complete series of scents and tastes whose beauty you once could not have imagined. But you cannot rush this development; it will come in its own time. In the sergeant's phrase: '*Wait* for it!'

One thing you can do to assist it. That is, control your smoking. All good wines, except sherries, are harmed by smoke. Your own palate is injured and made 'stupid' by

17

tobacco. Moreover, your neighbour, if he is a careful drinker, will have his wine partly ruined by your smoke. He will lose its bouquet entirely, and will lose part of its taste. I am told, but do not know from my own observation, that the late Stephen Gaselee, a fine Latin scholar and connoisseur of wine, used to travel around with four cardboard discs in his pocket, cut exactly to cover the tops of champagne, claret, hock and port glasses; whenever he was drinking good wine and someone near him lit a cigarette, he put the suitable card on top of his glass, and henceforward drank his wine with the card lifted (like the top of a mussel shell) just enough for him to insert his lips to the glass rim, glaring meanwhile at the boor or booress who was distressing him with ignorant exhalations. For smokers should note this fact: the smoke which is drawn into a smoker's mouth, the *blue* smoke, has a taste in it and is not disgusting. But the smoke which he blows out with his exhausted breath, the *brown* smoke, is repulsive. Test this some time when you are not yourself smoking: smell the two kinds of smoke off your wife or husband's cigarette. Or, more simply, go in, first thing in the morning, into a closed room where the old smoke of last night is still hanging in the air; shake out the curtains; breathe in what you find there.

Wine is made in all temperate and civilized countries, but in only eleven states is the product important enough to be worth speaking of here. (France, Germany, Spain, Italy, Hungary, Portugal, Switzerland, Yugoslavia, United States, South Africa, Australia.) All the best wines in the world still come from Western Europe, and it is interesting to note that the delightful smell, the 'bouquet' which is so much prized, is very rarely found elsewhere.

Sherry is a yellow-to-brown wine, used most frequently as an apéritif, except in its dark-brown form. Originally it owes its name to the Spanish town of Jerez de la Frontera. Plain 'sherry' should always be a Spanish wine or you are defrauded. A court judgment, however, allowed certain countries to continue to call their established wines of that type Australian Sherry, South African Sherry, or Cyprus Sherry – though not simply 'sherry'.

Claret is a derivation from the French word 'clairet', meaning a light red wine. The French word, out of use since the Middle Ages, was revived in 1950 by some enterprising St Emilion winegrowers, who distributed free under that name the contents of some barrels of a new type of pink quick-maturing wine, in the Place du Tertre at Montmartre; there were scenes of beatitude that afternoon which recalled a medieval Kermesse. That wine is well-flavoured, fresh, can be served cold, and doesn't mind being recorked. But it is not claret. Claret in English means red wine from the great district around Bordeaux, the largest and most venerable source of good red wines in the world. It may possibly be within the letter, if not the spirit, of the new law to apply it to other red wines of similar type from Australia, Chile, New York State, or where you will. The parallel white wine from Bordeaux is merely called 'white Bordeaux', or if it comes from a specified area 'Graves', 'Sauternes' or whatever it may be.

Burgundy is also an English word but 'Burgundy' alone should always mean a French wine, red or white, from the areas delimited by French law, and all – except Beaujolais – included in the old duchy of Burgundy. You will hear Wine Snobs saying that the areas outside what is called the 'Côte d'Or' – that is, the districts round Nuits and Beaune – do not produce true burgundy. This is nonsense. The chief areas concerned are, to the south, Mâcon and Beaujolais, the first originally part of the duchy and both explicitly included in the burgundy-producing districts by French law, and so entitled to the name. All that is true is that they are not usually as good as the Nuits and Beaune wines (when the latter are pure). Even this is not true of the area to the north, Chablis, which produces what many people think is the best white burgundy in the world. Burgundy is an English word, Chablis a French, but until the recent laws were introduced, both could be, and were, used indiscriminately on the British market for a heavy red or a dry – or not so dry – white wine, often without even the cautionary prefix 'Spanish' or 'Australian'. Since that became illegal many British wine drinkers have tasted true Chablis or Burgundy for the first time.

Champagne, by a separate court case of its own, made it illegal to apply it to anything but the sparkling product of Champagne, the area round Rheims in France. Others must call themselves Mousseux, Sparkling Moselle, Sparkling Californian White, or what they please. The still white wine of Champagne, a pleasant hard wine, and the not very remarkable still red, must now be called Coteaux Champenois.

Also in France, before we pass on, there are important wines (mostly white) of the *Loire,* such as Vouvray, and of the *Rhône,* which are mostly red, such as the Châteauneuf du Pape.

But the next great family of wines is what always used to be called *Rhenish.* The wines fall roughly into the categories of *Alsatians* or upper Rhine wines, of *Hocks,* a word which is used for the wines of the middle and lower Rhine (there are subdivisions here which will be described later) and of *Moselles,* wines grown along that tributary. They include the loveliest white wines in the world (the reds are trivial) and, never mind what the French say, all the best are in the German area. Hock is an English, not

20

a German word, and is sometimes used in such phrases as 'Australian hock' and 'Californian hock', to describe dry wines similar to Rhenish.

Port in Britain may not be used as a general descriptive word, because of treaties with Portugal dating back to 1702; it must refer only to the sweet, fortified red and white wines from the Douro valley, exported through Oporto. These treaties are, however, continually broken in conversation even in Britain by drinkers of Australian, South African or Cypriot wines of very similar type; and they are quite ignored in the States. Another famous dessert wine, less heavy, is *Tokay* from the district of that name in Hungary; other rivals are *Madeira*, from that island, *Marsala* from Sicily, and *Malaga* from that town in Spain. These are place-names: to attach them to Cape or Californian wines would be wrong.

In recent years Italian red and white wines have been exported in greater quantity, under closer control than ever before. They are plentiful and excellently fitted for drinking with pasta, meat and cheese. They are hardly ever great wines but there is reason to believe that they will become much better. That is true also of Spanish and Portuguese table wines, of the wines of Yugoslavia and probably even those of Greece.

All these countries have both red and white wines for drinking with meals. After-dinner wines (except port), however, are not so divided; they are mostly yellow-to-brown and their colour usually darkens as they grow sweeter

One can tell which family, so to speak, a wine belongs to by a quick glance at the bottle. Rhenish wines have long, thin, graceful tapering bottles, which contain about a glass less than ordinary bottles. Burgundies come in wide bottles with sloping shoulders – or, to be more exact, no shoulders at all. Clarets and the equivalent white wines are in narrower bottles with squarer shoulders, the most common type of wine bottle. Ports and sherries have similar bottles, usually with a flat bottom instead of the cone which rises into the glass of other wine bottles. Champagnes and sparkling wine bottles are like burgundies with thicker glass, wired-on corks, and tinfoil all down the neck. Italian wines sometimes come in rounded flasks set in straw cases, which ought to contain a full litre, a third more than a bottle.

What is inside these bottles is, however, more usefully listed for the beginner in three classes, according to how and when they are drunk:

(1) Wines taken as apéritifs, before meals.

(2) Wines taken with meals, called 'table wines'.

(3) Wines taken at the end of meals, called 'dessert wines'.

The first, *apéritif wines* are best served cold. Pale and medium sherries are excellent appetizers, and are always better cold. So, too, are the various 'Quinquinas', Cap Corses, Pernods, Byrrhs, Clacquesins, and so on, which tourists and the less wise Frenchmen pour into their insides. These latter indeed are so strong that it is best to put ice *into* them (which should not be done to real wine) to diminish their crudity. Also the very best of all cocktails, champagne, should always be served cold, as should too the sparkling Moselles, Saumurs and such which imitate it. 'Cold' in this connection means cool in the mouth. It does not mean iced so long and heavily that the wine jars your palate like a lump of ice-cream and all its taste is frozen.

Many people prefer to classify champagne as a table wine and drink it, when they can afford to, with their food; the French frequently drink it at the end of a meal.

(Always, still, it must be cold.) There is nothing against this; it is a matter of taste. But I have always found it inconvenient though flattering to be offered champagne throughout the meal unless my host had the Japanese custom of considering resounding belches as complimentary. Even if you take the precaution of releasing some of the gas by twirling in the glass a wooden stick called a swizzlestick which horrifies champagne enthusiasts, still enough remains in the wine to cause unwelcome congestion in the stomach, when it is mixed with solid food.

Table wines are clarets, burgundies, and Rhenish; and wines of those types. They are red (which means anything from pale scarlet to purple), white (which means yellow), or rosé (which means pink). Red wines are made from black grapes; white from white grapes, or from black grapes whose juice has been run off without the skins being allowed to enter the vats. Rosé is made in various ways (including the crude mixing together of red and white), but properly it should either be produced from grapes with light-red skins, or black grapes whose skins have been very briefly mashed with the must. White wines should be cold, in the sense of cool in the mouth, as already explained. Rosé wines, of which there are few and none of outstanding quality, should be served cool too. Red wines should be at the temperature of the room, or it might be more exact to say, of your mouth (for some people keep their rooms far too hot). If in doubt, remember it is better to have red wines too cool than too hot, for by holding the glass in your hand you can easily take off the chill, whereas wine which has been overheated and partly cooked never quite recovers its character. If you have a good red wine, it is best to bring it up from the cellar an hour at least before drinking it. Supposing you have improvidently forgotten to do so, then for the majority of wines it is safe to plunge the bottle into mildly warm (not hot) water, for five minutes. You will find this practice denounced in the manuals; ignore them. Only the oldest and most delicate wines can be injured by it; on evenings when you propose to drink such wines, then you must remember to bring them up early; and that is all there is to it.

Most of this advice is mere common sense. It is obvious that it would be bad for wine to freeze it or to boil it. But there is one rule which a newcomer cannot be expected to know, and that is: 'Give the wine time to breathe.' As soon as the cork is drawn the air begins to make certain chemical changes in the wine. It brings out both its taste and its bouquet; the longer it is allowed to work upon the wine the more it will bring them out. Eventually, of course, it will take them all away and leave only a flat vinegarish liquid. But pretty well every wine is improved by being given an hour in which to breathe, and so far from this being a precaution necessary for good wines only, it is even more important for indifferent wines. A coarse Algerian or Australian is markedly improved if the cork is drawn (and not replaced) as much as six hours beforehand. I have known a case when twenty-four hours was needed. This rule does not apply only to table wines, but to all wines (except sparkling wines, of course), and to full sherry in particular, which does not only stay for days in a decanter undamaged but actually improves. Why this is no one can say; it is contrary to reason and to the habits of all other wines. But that it does is vouched for by too many people for it to be an illusion.

The only exception is very old wine which may be so fragile that its taste, together with its perfume, will evaporate into the air in a matter of minutes. But you are not often likely to be offered wines 30 or 40 years old, I suppose.

Dessert wines should be served at room temperature. The best-known dessert wine is port; next come, as has been said, madeira, Tokay, marsala, brown sherry and malaga. Except for Tokay, they are not 'natural' wines, they are fortified and extra sugar or syrup is usually added. The Danes and Swedes used to keep them in refrigerators and serve them from bottles with ice on them. This is a Viking barbarity; the taste of the wines is almost entirely destroyed by it, and a grand vintage port tastes the same as a Fruity Invalid.

It is a good habit to handle all wine bottles gently. No bottle at all is improved by being brandished like an Indian club, and the older red wines are definitely harmed. They deposit a 'crust' within the bottle, made of impurities in the wine which it has got rid of as it matured. The heavier the wine, usually, the more marked the crust: port crust is sometimes a film that can be held in the hand. If by jerking the bottle about you break up this crust and send it floating around in the wine again you undo for the moment the work of years; the wine will look muddy as you pour it out and will taste muddy too. Even white wines sometimes throw a sand-like deposit which is better undisturbed.

Sometimes it is impossible to avoid shaking. If you order from a wine merchant or buy at an auction wine which has been several years in bottle, the railway or the carter is sure to shake it thoroughly. Very often a man has tasted a delightful wine at his wine-merchant's, opened it when it arrived, and wondered why on earth he bought the dull and dusty drink. In such a case, always let the wine lie undisturbed on its side for at least a month – more if you think it has been badly shaken or is particularly delicately-flavoured; then it will recover.

Most wine manuals, and even books of household

management, contain tables showing what wines must be drunk with particular foods. These are by no means reliable; indeed, by nature they cannot be. People's mouths are not alike, because their chemical constitution is different; the only safe rule is, once again, 'Do what you like. Follow the guidance of your palate.' Later in this book will be printed, with all reserve, one of these guides. But here, where we are dealing with general principles, there are only two worth remembering, and on which almost all palates will agree. The first is that red wine does not usually go well with fish. The second is that sweet wines do not go well with any 'main dish', fish or meat or game. Avoiding these two combinations, you can fairly safely try anything. Distrust positive commands – even the commonest of all, to 'serve white wines with fish.' This instruction, copied from a book, has induced trusting readers to bring out a Sauternes with fish, which is as eccentric as eating chocolate sauce with whiting. The chief condition required of a wine that is to be drunk with fish (including shellfish) is that it should not be sweet: therefore, pick on a white burgundy, a hock, a moselle, an Alsatian, or a Graves which is in fact dry (most are not). Keep the Sauternes and Barsacs for the end of the meal, with the fruit, when their sweetness will be less cloying and your palate can attend to their almost childish series of scented flavours, like a succession of heavy flowers held under your nose. If you haven't a dry white wine for your fish, do what your grandfather did – take a glass of not-too-thin sherry with it. (Don't, by the way, trouble to serve wine with soup; if for some reason you think you must, serve a medium sherry, not a very dry one; or a madeira might be better.)

Apart from this, do as you please. You do not *have* to serve red wine with meat or game. A good white wine will do excellently. You do not, even, have to serve white wine with fish. Several times in St Emilion itself my hosts have served me with their own red wines with lampreys, most fishy fish, and they have been quite agreeable; I admit I would not, however, like to try doing this myself. Fish usually does make red wine taste sour.

Vintage years provide a subject for discussion which greatly abashes the unlearned; it is the Wine Snob's favourite, next to the especially delicate wine from an obscure district that he and the Marquis de la Chose practically alone know of. And there is, in fact, some useful knowledge here, but it can easily be condensed. Firstly, there are no years at all in sherry. Sherries are blended. The word 'Solera' with a date means only that a butt was started in such a year; it has no significance beyond assuring you the firm has been a long time in business. Secondly, there is no need to know about the vintages of ports and champagnes. In both these cases, the firms never date the wines of any years but really good years; the others they blend. If a wine is dated, then it is bound to be a good year. You may safely, if it gives you any pleasure, say in an authoritative voice: 'Roederer '55? Taylor '27? Very good years,' if you see them on the list, for if they had not been very good the firms would not have dated them. All you need to remember is that champagne will not keep, and port will die in forty years. But there is no need to remember all the years which are entered on those agreeable little cards which wine merchants will give you to put in your pocket-book (or even those in the longer list which is printed later on in this book).

There are only a few years which are worth memorising, and that more for the pleasure of being able to take part in elegant conversations about vintages than for any practical use you are likely to make of them. In many wine books you will find rhapsodies over great vintages of the past – 1906 and 1911 were famous for burgundies, 1921 was fabulous for hocks, 1929 clarets have never been equalled. True, or at least possible; but of no importance; for these wines can no longer be bought, or if they can be found they will almost certainly be too old to drink.

For most practical purposes only the post-1955 vintages are now worth remembering; and any older are scarce. Those of 1959, 1961, 1962 and 1970 were all outstanding in almost all the wine regions; 1964, 1966 and 1971 uneven but generally good. The Rhine, Moselle and Rhône wines of 1971 were extremely fine. Some of the great clarets of 1961 are still not completely ready to drink; 1962 and 1964 are; 1970 promises to mature early. Beaujolais, of course, should be drunk young; even the best of it will hardly improve after three years.

The last hurdle over which you might fall is made of glass; it can be made to vanish even more easily than the others. There are five main traditional shapes for wineglasses. A sherry glass is shaped like a capital V; a claret glass has a wide cup like the socket of an acorn; a port glass is similar but smaller; a champagne glass is flat and broad; a hock glass tall and with a cup of coloured glass, so:

But there is no need to know these; for, to wine drinkers, not one is of any importance; not one of them improves the wine in any way at all. There is only one satisfactory type of wine glass, and it will serve for any kind of wine. It is colourless, rather tulip-shaped, and the upper rim of the cup narrows.

It looks like this:

and you will find it used in any intelligent wine bar or restaurant. If it is thin, it is pleasanter to the lips, but its thickness has no other importance. Even a small tumbler whose upper edges are pinched together will do better than any of the traditional Victorian shapes illustrated above. These shapes are sometimes very pretty to look at; some wineglasses are delightful as glass, and if you collect glass, collect them. But for wine drinking they have nearly every fault.

The reasons for their existence are economic, and not very creditable to their devisers. The sherry glass is an innkeepers' trick. It makes the quantity of wine look much more than it is. Fill up that V-shaped glass two-thirds of the way, and you have much less than two-thirds of a glassful of wine. The coloured cup for hock and white wine glasses is due to the fact that in the Victorian age white wines were often carelessly made, and specks of dust and solid matter would be found floating in them. The coloured glass concealed this: you can tell the Wine Snob that his hock glasses have to be coloured because his wine is dirty. The champagne glass is broad and flat for ostentation's sake; all the restaurant can see what you are drinking. No wine merchant uses it nowadays. For taste and taste alone, champagne is best drunk in beer tankards, believe it or

not. But then of course people may think you are only
drinking beer.

The reasons why the glass illustrated here is in fact
best, are interesting. They involve a discussion of the whole
art and pleasure of drinking wine. Consider: for what
purpose do you drink wine? To get drunk? Then you are
a foolish fellow, and should not be reading this book. Besides, it is a very poor instrument for getting drunk; if
that is your object, try a mixture of 60 per cent. whisky
and 40 per cent vodka. It will do the trick quicker and
more thoroughly than anything else. For your health's
sake, and to make your food more digestible? That is a
good reason, but there quite probably are some pepsin tab-
lets or something of the sort which would serve. Yet no one
in his senses would regard them as a substitute for wine.
In fact, wine is drunk for immediate pleasure first, and to
attain after that a general feeling of well-being, a *euphoria*
as the doctors call it, in which the mind is placid but lively,
the emotions are friendly, and the body calm and satisfied.
In wine drinking, consequently, four faculties are involved:
Sight, Smell, Taste, Digestion. Digestion is not under our
control – or, rather, all that we can do is to interfere with
it by mixing drinks or drinking to excess. But the other
three are, and they are, curiously enough, connected
directly with the type of glass used.

This is the way to drink wine.

Pour the wine, steadily and not splashily, into the type
of glass named, filling it only two-thirds full. Then use the
faculty of *sight*; look at it. This is why the glass should
be colourless. You have paid for, and should enjoy, the
fine yellow of a big hock or of a sauternes, the pale straw-
like yellow of a manzanilla sherry, the dark heavy red of
a burgundy, or that curious fading colour of an ageing
claret. At the edge of the glass in this case the red of the

wine fades almost to grey, to colourlessness. Observe, too, if the wine is muddy, and not, as it should be, brilliantly clear. If the red is turbid or the white has specks floating in it, you have received a warning already.

Next, use the sense of *smell*. Hold the glass in your hand and rotate the wine gently. (This is why it must only be filled two-thirds full.) Then hang your nose over the edge of it and sniff. This is why the glass must come together at the rim, to collect the smell and present it respectfully to your nostrils. The Victorian glasses dissipate it into the room. It is difficult not to be lyrical over the bouquet of a good wine. Tokay smells like green grass and weeds, trampled underfoot in a lush meadow. A full burgundy has a scent so strong it may make you dizzy; in its compound of flavours you can imagine violets and blackberries. A hock or moselle smells like a large bouquet of midsummer flowers. A claret is usually more delicate: its scents seem (but this may be fanciful) to succeed one another, like a chorus mincing across the stage. Moreover, the bouquet, too, may be a warning as well as a pleasure. A nasty wine, such as a bad sherry (or, for that matter, a murderous whisky) tells your nose before you taste it. It stinks and you know there is villainy. Pour it into the potted plant and ask your host, next round, for gin.

Thirdly, use the sense of *taste*. Raise the glass to your mouth, take a small mouthful and roll it round your mouth. Let it irrigate the teeth and give the taste-buds of your tongue and palate time to notice and consider the first and second tastes that a wine usually has. Hold it in the mouth long enough to breathe in and out once through the nose. Then swallow, and you will often find that there is a third and last taste that it gives you as a farewell as it passes your tonsils. Then, after a moment of consideration, take a second larger mouthful if the wine deserves it. That is why the glass must be reasonably large; thimbles are a nuisance at this point.

All this may sound a lot of trouble; and it is true that not all wines deserve it. There are wines so ordinary that they only deserve to be bolted, as there is food so dull that it only deserves to be gobbled – boiled cod or coley, for example. But even with indifferent wines the careful drinker will stop for a moment to classify them, so to speak, before he puts them down. For the rest, all this procedure is merely a way of increasing your pleasure. It requires attention, but so do all pleasures. In fact, attentiveness is part of the nature of pleasure; an unobserved pleasure is not a pleasure at all.

*   *   *

To summarize, as promised, in postcard length; the necessary minimum of knowledge about wine is this:

Don't serve red wines with fish.

Don't serve sweet wines with main dishes.

Cool in the mouth: White wines and before-dinner wines.

Room temperature: Red wines and after-dinner wines.

Uncork wine at least an hour before, if you can.

Drink from a glass like this:

Pour gently, rotate in the glass and smell before swallowing.

Years to remember: 1959, 1961, 1962, 1964, 1966, 1970, 1971.

Don't smoke over wines.

Follow your own taste, not others'.

33

2. 'The Second Lesson'

Wine merchants – Cleaning the palate – Labels:
(1) Shippers; (2) 'Appellation Contrôlée', with
list of French Regions; (3) Château-bottled;
(4) Grape-names – Fuller list of vintages – Un-
corking, serving and decanting – How to get, and
remedy, a 'thick head' – Menus with suitable
wines – How much per head? – Cellars and
cellar substitutes – A specimen balanced cellar –
Punch and cups.

A MAN who wants to buy wine for himself does not have to have a wine merchant. Fifty years ago it was good advice to all but the smallest buyers to choose one reliable firm and deal only with it; and there are still in some provincial towns in England, and in London too, pleasant, rather dark and small rooms with smooth old furniture, which are neither quite offices nor quite shops, tenanted by mellowed and usually quiet men 'of a certain age', neither quite tradesmen nor quite professional advisers. These men are the élite of the wine trade, there is no doubt; anyone who purchases wine consistently will before long find that he has made at least one of them his consultant and friend. But this sedate trade may be near to extinction. Tanner of Shrewsbury; Christophers, Dolamore, Berry Bros & Rudd, Corney & Barrow, G. F. Grant, Loeb, and Reynier of London; and best known of all, Avery of Bristol still exist; but others equally famous have been swallowed by enormous multiple firms, and though their names are still on the doors they have lost their independence. 'Allied Breweries' whose centre was Ind Coope in 1966 controlled a full dozen such. 'International Distillers and Vintners', one of whose main constituents was Gilbey's, issued a chart of its independants which looked like a genealogy of German princelets in the *Almanach de Gotha*. 'Traders' was another bloc. Though the principals are often my friends, and though I know that their actions correspond to the Marxist law of the concentration of capital, I cannot conceal that I think this development has been on the whole evil; it has not even secured us the commonest benefit of standardisation, the elimination of fraud. All the advice that can be usefully given to a consumer is to examine the wine shops in his own town, eliminate those whose stocks are almost identical, drink a few bottles, and make his own choice. In any case, he should spread his buying around, and get on several mailing lists. There is no more consoling reading on a wet day than a wine merchant's catalogue, and the phrases that the writers use to describe their wares are rich and unusual. Sometimes they are obscure: one favourite, 'a wine of great vinosity' is almost meaningless. Sometimes they are terrifying: 'QUIMPORTO: A mixture of quinine, beef-tea and fine port. Preferred by connoisseurs' was a recommendation I noted down in London before the second world war.

In the merchant's office, in the multiple shop, and for that matter in the restaurant, the wine-lover has to make his choice on limited evidence. He will not usually, except in the first case, be able to taste. (Bread and salt, a dry biscuit, or a small square of common cheese are the best means of cleaning the palate before tasting wine, at a merchant's or at table. In restaurants a waiter will frequently offer you the first drop of a red wine to approve just when you are gulping the tail-end of an oily sardine;

use bread and salt then.) Nor will the label on the wine bottle tell him a great deal until he is familiar with the names of quite a number of individual wines. But it will tell him certain important things: (1) The name of the shipper; (2) the name of the region; (3) whether the wine is estate-bottled or not; (4) the grape used, but this may not be equally important.

(1) The name of the shipper – or, at any rate, the exporting house – is of first importance in sherry, port, and champagne; it is of considerable importance in burgundy; it is of less importance elsewhere. Names worth remembering in the three first cases will be given in the later sections, but a drinker soon learns his own preferences.

(2) The name of the region is usually the most important information to be found upon a label. In France, Germany and Italy strict and detailed laws control the use of regional names, which is one reason why these countries are producing the best wines in the world. The South Africans who name their wine Constantia and the Californians who name theirs Napa Valley have set their feet upon the same ladder of honest wine-making. For the foundation of a *vigneron's* honesty is pride in his own product; he is not producing a fine wine unless and until he can insist on saying: 'This is my wine, it comes from my vineyards; see, their name is on it, and it is not adulterated with other wine, for that would destroy its particular quality.'

On a French wine the words to look for are 'Appellation Contrôlée.' They mean that the name has been applied in conformity with the French law on appellations. This law does not merely insist that the wine shall come from the area named; it also requires that it shall have been made in accordance with some very detailed conditions.

The law does not indeed ensure quality – for not even a Chamber of Deputies can issue orders to the weather – but it prevents some known methods of deterioration. For example, among the conditions which must be observed before a man may label his wine 'St Emilion' are: firstly, the territorial limits which are described down to separate parcels of land; secondly, that crops with more than 20 per cent. of injured or 'ill' grapes must be sorted individually; thirdly, that the actual wine-making must follow local customs contained in earlier statutes; fourthly, that only certain named vines may be used and they must be planted at certain distances; fifthly, that they must be trained and pruned by the Guyot method, under limitations which are so abstruse as to be untranslatable; and sixthly, that the 'must' shall contain at least 178 grammes of sugar per litre and after fermentation must produce not less than $10\frac{1}{2}$ degrees of alcohol. (A 'degree' of alcohol, by the way, is not the same as a percentage of alcohol. Table wines vary between 7 and 15 degrees usually, and 10 to 11 is a common figure for French ordinaires, but wines below 9 degrees are rarely worth exporting. In Bordeaux and the other areas in which great quantities of wine are produced the degrees figure is taken as a rough guide to quality, and prices in the '*Prisunic*' and other French shops which sell every-day wines are an exact reflection of alcoholic strength.)

Some 'appellations' are confined to one area, such as the small town of Cassis on the Mediterranean which produces agreeable white wines; some cover great tracts of land, such as 'Bordeaux'. But in the latter case they are subdivided: a wine called 'Bordeaux' merely comes from the Bordeaux area and satisfies certain general tests, but a wine called Barsac comes from that small district within the Bordeaux area and meets much more detailed provisions. Here is a list of the chief 'appellations contrôlées' in France with their best known subdivisions.

BURGUNDY (Bourgogne): Main subdivisions, north to south: Chablis, Côte d'Or (Côte de Nuits and Côte de Beaune), Mâcon, Beaujolais.

CHAMPAGNE: Coteaux champenois.

CÔTES DU JURA: Arbois, Château Chalon, Seyssel.

CÔTES DU RHÔNE: Côte Rôtie, Hermitage, Châteauneuf du Pape, Tavel, Condrieu, Gigondas.

CENTRE AND WEST (LOIRE) – West to east: Muscadet, Anjou, Saumur, Vouvray, Sancerre, Pouilly. (There is another Pouilly in Burgundy.)

BORDEAUX: Médoc, Haut Médoc, Graves, Sauternes, Entre-deux-mers, St Emilion, Pomerol, Fronsac, Bourg, Blaye.

Isolated 'Appellations': Cahors, Cassis, Jurançon, Gaillac, and several others. The French attach importance to a group of sweet wines at the eastern end of the Pyrenees: Maury, Rivesaltes, Côtes de Roussillon, Banyuls (north to south).

Of recent years there have appeared on the tables of the better French restaurants wines which bear a special and easily recognizable label containing the letters V.D.Q.S. These stand for *vin délimité de qualité supérieure*, and though the wines are not up to the standard of the 'A.C.' wines they are a great deal better than the ordinary *pinard* of the estaminets. There is no point in giving a full list of them (and they are anyway added to fairly easily), but some which you are likely to see on your travels and which are a guarantee of pretty fair quality are these:

Rosé de Béarn, St Pourçain sur Sioule, Cour-Cheverny, Côtes du Forez, Gros Plant Nantais, Côtes de Toul, Côtes de Provence, Costières du Gard, Bugey, Roussette de Bugey, Coteaux de Pierrevert, Tursan, Côtes d'Auvergne, Côtes du Marmandais, d'Estaing Minervois, Corbières, and Sauvignon de Saint Bris.

(3) The words 'Mise au Château' or 'Mis en bouteilles au Château' with a date, mean that the proprietor that year considered some or all of his wine good enough to bottle it himself and sell it under his own personal guarantee. The cork, in this case, should also have his name or mark upon it when it is withdrawn. Some thieving wine-waiters have been known to trade in branded corks. Therefore, when a cork is handed to you in a restaurant, look at it closely. Don't just be content to see the brand is on it; pinch it. Make sure that it is resilient and damp; it should be well saturated by recent contact with wine and not have had a chance to get dry and hard. Château bottling is a guarantee of authenticity but it also means an increase in price, for wine is much easier to transport in barrels.

In earlier editions I advised purchasers in the United States to attach importance to château bottling (or 'domaine bottling' or 'Originalabfüllung'; they are all the same), but not the British. An exposure in the British press at the end of 1966 showed how simple-minded I had been. Mediterranean wines of all kinds were being blended to the distributors' orders, and labelled 'Nuits St Georges' 'Beaujolais' or whatever else they demanded. French exporters would send out genuine burgundies to acquiescent British firms without the Government certificates, which they then used for other wines. Names like 'Clos de X' or 'Château Y' were invented and stuck on to bottles that might contain any old mixture. How wide and deep the corruption was I cannot say; but there is some villainy in every profitable trade. Certainly it showed the need for the E.E.C. control which now ensures, as nearly as possible, that a bottle labelled with an 'official' place-name does contain the wine of that place.

(4) Some labels have the names of grapes on them. Hungarian bottles have 'Furmint' and Alsatian 'Sylvaner' or 'Gewurztraminer', for example; or 'Riesling' almost anywhere, from Hunter River to Livermore, where white wine is produced. The label means that the wine is made from grapes off the vine of that name. This is, in practice, of little interest to anyone but experts in the trade. It gives no guide whatever to the taste of the wine in the bottle; there is an abundance of Rieslings, correctly so described, which range in taste from fifth-rate to excellent. The family of the vine is only one, and not the most important, of the sources of goodness in wine. Put a Californian vine in the soil of Bordeaux, in the Bordeaux climate and under the Bordeaux sun, and it will produce a Médoc or a Graves; take a Bordeaux vine to Australia and it will produce the usual strong flagon wine.

The obstinacy of the Alsatians in naming their wines by vines instead of places is one reason, I believe, why they missed the chance that they had to establish themselves in British and American favour immediately after the second world war, when hocks were unavailable or unreliable. A customer would drink a 'Sylvaner' and find it charming; he would buy another 'Sylvaner', and it would be a thin, white-faced, sharp, spinsterish liquid totally unlike the first. He concluded that there was no relying on Alsatian labels, and waited for the German wines to come back.

The vintages of wines are a much more useful guide; and here, as promised, is a fuller list of good years. In using it, two things must be noted. Firstly, any information about good and bad years is only approximate. In poor years, there are always certain vineyards which have escaped whatever ruined the rest of the crop. I have drunk excellent '44s and '54s, but both of these were classed as poor years. In good years, there are similarly certain vineyards which have had no luck and their produce is nothing more than an ordinaire; I have drunk a dismal Chateau Haut Brion of 1928. Secondly, wine improves unequally, partly according to the size of its container. A half-bottle develops less character and body than a whole bottle, and it also dies sooner. A magnum (two bottles) lasts longer, and develops slightly better than a bottle. This is not usually true of the monsters called a double magnum (4 bottles) and jeroboam (6 bottles – 4 in champagne) still less of the absurdities with Old Testament names (Rehoboam, Methusaleh, Salamanazar, Balthasar, Nebuchadnezzar) running up to 20 bottles. I suspect that the reason may sometimes be that the wine has not in fact matured in these carboys, but ordinary bottles have just been poured into them. Anyway, here is a guide to the years which in my experience can be regarded as good. For the reasons which I have just given, I am not going to try to classify them more elaborately, and I am omitting, deliberately, all pre-1959 vintages, except for port. Some 1945 and 1947 table wines may conceivably come your way which have survived and are splendid; there may indeed even be earlier wines; but they will be rarities, and rash would be the man who bought them without tasting. Even now, in 1976, it is wise to be cautious in buying vintages before 1959, with the exception of 1953 (if you can find any of that). 1947, 1950, 1952 and 1955 were all in their day good vintages, but they are weakening even in clarets, the longest-lived of all table wines. Wine-making was extensively modernized – it is a matter of opinion whether the word should in fact be 'improved' as the trade claimed – as soon as the war was over, and among the results of the changes was quicker maturing which, as always, means quicker death.

RED BORDEAUX: 1959, 1961, 1962, 1966, 1970, 1971.
WHITE BORDEAUX: 1959, 1961, 1962, 1967, 1970.
RED BURGUNDY: 1961, 1962, 1964, 1966, 1969, 1971, 1972.
WHITE BURGUNDY: 1961, 1964, 1966, 1969, 1971, 1973.
LOIRE WINES: 1967, 1969, 1970, 1971.
RHENISH: 1964, 1966, 1969, 1971.
CHAMPAGNE: 1961, 1962, 1964, 1966, 1969, 1970.
RHONE WINES: 1961, 1964, 1965, 1966, 1969, 1970, 1971, 1972.
PORT: 1948, 1950, 1955, 1960, 1963, 1967, 1970.

Time is of course cutting away at this table, which, like all of its kind, is a table of mortality. Do not rely upon it, and remember the aphorism most neglected in this country of England, where Wine Snobs have made a fetish of vintages: 'More good wine is wasted by being drunk too late than too soon'.

To serve your wine, when you have chosen it and brought it up from the cellar, you need a corkscrew and a towel or napkin. Now, when you hold the bottle between your knees, grasping the neck with one hand and pulling on the corkscrew with the other, always wrap the bottle's neck in a napkin. It is only one bottle in two hundred – what am I saying? less even than that – which has a flaw in it. But that bottle will slice deeply into your hand, just where the thumb joins the palm. Your blood will splash all over the room, you will spoil the wine, and you may lose the use of your thumb and finger. Alternatively, you may avoid grasping the bottle at all by using one of those patent corkscrews, with outspread wings or tubular screws which can be fixed on top of the bottle as it stands on the table; there is also a corkscrew – called 'the butler's friend' – very good for old corks, which has two blades that slip down the side of the cork, but this is more difficult to manage. There is, too, a strange device incorporating a sort of hypodermic syringe which injects gas underneath the cork and makes it leap out of the bottle; if it applies pressure on a flaw in the bottle, the result can be alarming: eye surgeons do not recommend it. Always choose a corkscrew whose spiral is flat and broad. Long, narrow blades, such as are often found in multiple pocket-knives, make a hole in soft corks and pull them away in pieces, scattering scraps of cork into the wine.

The sort of bed, metal or wicker, called a 'cradle' is almost entirely, in my view, ostentation. It is supposed to make pouring the wine smoother, but the process of getting the bottle into the cradle shakes the wine more than any ordinarily careful pouring would; in my experience, too, most cradles do not hold the bottle still but allow it to jiggle. The only true use of a cradle is for moving a very old wine from its place in a bin without standing it upright at all; the cork must be drawn out sideways and the bottle held immovable. This hardly ever happens. When the waiter brings you your wine in a cradle in a restaurant, then your guests and the neighbouring tables know that you have chosen an expensive wine, but that small-souled gratification is usually all that the device offers.

All wines, except very ancient wines, may be decanted. Decanting is never harmful, and never essential. The oldest port can be poured gently from its bottle, leaving the crust undisturbed, the newest red Australian will be aerated by being decanted. Red wines and sherries gain most by being decanted; white wines are hardly improved at all. Before decanting, wipe the lip and inside of the neck of the bottle with a cloth, to remove any dirt or cork-scraps. See that the decanter is clean and dry, with no musty smell; if you have any doubt, rinse round the inside with a very little of the wine you are going to use, and throw away. When decanting, hold the decanter in your left hand, and the bottle in your right, between your eyes and the light. Hold them at an angle like a gable, or the roofs of a house, so that the wine flows steadily but not too fast. If the wine is one in which you expect a deposit, watch it as it pours out, and the moment any turbidity or muddiness appears, stop. Put the rest of the bottle aside and if there is anything more than a spoonful left you can probably use it for cooking.

In serving drink, there is one old-established rule that proves itself yearly in innumerable splitting headaches. Don't mix drinks. It is sometimes claimed that wine can follow beer; but not vice versa. After beer, whisky is safer; after wine, brandy; and, after cider, drink applejack or calvados. Mix these three staples and your liver and your head will punish you gleefully in the morning. The safest of all rules is to keep strictly not only to one substance, but to one wine. It is remarkable how much a man can take, without harm, of the same claret, the same burgundy, or the same champagne; he is liable to pass out the moment he changes from it.

If you suspect you are going to exceed, take a spoonful of olive oil (or other oil) before you start; it will protect the stomach and delay intoxication. If you think you have exceeded, drink when you come home (if you can bear it) a glass of cold milk; in the morning take an alkaline effervescence like an 'alka-seltzer', walk a good distance

44

in the open air, and at eleven o'clock try a vile-tasting Italian compound called Fernet Branca.

In any case, when you exceed, beware of the fortified wines – the ports, sweet sherries and madeiras. Their duplicate excess of sugar and high alcoholic content will put a cruel strain on your liver. Our ancestors, who spent whole days fox hunting, were three-bottle men, no doubt, but we don't live their lives. Also, they died young, purple or yellow, gouty, savage-tempered and inflamed; the memoirs of the eighteenth century are full of the results of port drinking.

But these are the paths of folly; the path of wisdom is to drink wine sedately with the food that becomes it. There is, as has been said, no 'rule' as to what wine to serve with any one course. Your own palate must be your own guide. But for those who do not yet trust their judgment, and still wish to entertain friends, here are some combinations which have generally been found palatable:

With	*Try*
Hors d'oeuvre	Dry or medium sherry.
Oysters	Chablis, light white dry wines – Moselle, Alsatian, burgundy.
Soup	Nothing, or a medium sherry, or a dry Madeira.
Fish	A dry white Bordeaux or burgundy, or a Rhenish wine, or indeed any Yugoslav or other white wine which isn't sweet.
Chicken and other white meats.	A claret, a light burgundy, or a solid white wine like a Montrachet.
Red meat	Any red wine.

45

With	*Try*
Game..	A heavier red wine, a full St Emilion claret, a solid burgundy, or a strong Rhône wine like the Châteauneuf du Pape.
Curry..	Beer, ginger-beer, iced water, fruit cup; but not wine.
Chinese food..	Pale yellow hot tea with no milk or sugar.
Danish and Swedish food.	Aquavit and lager alternately for as long as you can sit up to table.
Sweets and desserts ..	Sauternes and such; or a rich hock.
Cheese	Practically any wine at all. Cheese has the property of bringing out the flavour of wine unless it is so corrupt as to kill any other taste. But even so, Roquefort is called 'the drunkard's biscuit'. Very nearly perfect dietetically, besides being as delightful as it is simple, is a meal consisting of a bottle of claret, cheese, fresh brown bread, butter and an undressed salad.
Fruit and nuts	Tokay, port, madeira, brown sherry, Sauternes, rich hock.

Most manuals will tell you that rosé and champagne can be served throughout a meal, and with anything. This is true only to the extent that there is no food that they particularly clash with. But there are objections to this advice. Rosé is a sweetish, silly wine for careless drinking at a tennis-party or such; at a serious meal with elder persons it is likely to seem tasteless, and for some it will be acid in the stomach later. Champagne, besides being expensive and ostentatious, doesn't agree with everyone as a drink with a meal, and even those who are devoted to it are likely to hanker after at least one glass of red wine before they rise from the table.

Before serving your guests in any case pour a few drops into your own glass and taste. This is no longer a demonstration that your wine is not poisoned; it is merely to ensure that any scraps of cork or wax go into your glass and not theirs, and to give you an opportunity to make sure that you have not by any accident got hold of a bad bottle.

If you are giving a long formal dinner with several wines, there are three rules of common sense: serve better wines after ordinary wines, sweet after dry, strong after gentle – not the other way round. The guests at Cana were half-drunk and their opinion was valueless. Sometimes you will hear a wine spoken of as 'corked'; strictly, this word should only be used of wine which has drawn an unpleasant flavour from a bad cork. More commonly the musty flavour which it describes is due to a spore of mildew which has got into the wine before bottling and multiplied. However, the lax use of the word is now universal, and there is no point in trying to change it. There is no cure for 'corked' wine; it is useless.

How much you allow to your guests depends upon your estimate of their habits. For a man and his wife not accustomed to drinking wine, a half bottle may be enough, but for most wine lovers a bottle between two would seem to be a comfortable allowance, and a bottle each too much. But the amount does not increase arithmetically with the number of your guests; if you are six in all who look on the whole 'half-bottle men', you may not need to drink three whole bottles. Even so, it is wise to have a spare bottle, unopened, as a reserve.

This advice on serving wine assumes that you have a cellar. If you have one, dark, underground and about 55 degrees Fahrenheit, you are lucky, and need do no more than keep your wine on its side there, in boxes or more preferably in bins. But if you have none, then you must search in your house for a place with the qualities needed in a cellar. These are: stillness, so that the wine will not be shaken; relative darkness, for strong light may harm it; unvarying coolness, for warmth and change mature it too fast; room, so that the bottles may lie on their side – otherwise the corks may dry up, shrivel, and let in the air. Cupboards, not in living-rooms, if they are deep enough, will serve. The empty space underneath the stairs in small houses is often just the place. Air-raid shelters (disused) are frequently admirable.

What should one put in his cellar, large or small? First of all, no spirits. No spirit improves in bottle; after twenty years in your cellar it will be no better. So let the wine merchant keep your whisky, rum and brandy for you; stock only what you need immediately; Nor would I advise keeping more than a single or two bottles of champagne or sparkling wine, in case of unexpected births or marriages. They don't improve and may go flat in bottle; they are expensive and lock up a good deal of capital. Here is a suggested cellar of, say, five dozen bottles for a beginning. I am suggesting the proportions alone, of course; the actual quantity is a matter between you and your banking account. It is pleasant to enter all your purchases in a 'cellar book' (rule it out in five columns headed: *Date and amount of Purchase; Wine; Year; Merchant; Verdict*); it makes agreeable reading in later years, and will prevent you repeating a mistake.

I would suggest then:

Six bottles of sherry – three dry, three medium.

Six bottles of dessert wines – four of port, one of madeira, one of sweet sherry.

Twelve bottles of burgundy – half cheap, half slightly better.

Twelve bottles of claret, similarly divided.

Twelve bottles of table white wines – white burgundies, dry Graves, moselles, and so on. Possibly include three bottles of rosé, if you like it.

Six bottles of sweet white wine.

Two champagnes or sparkling wine, for sudden rejoicing.

Four single bottles of really good vintage table wines, for dinners which are special occasions, which no one but yourself may open.

Two final remarks: One: remember, no wine need ever be wasted. This is not a cookery book, but there are many cookery books (for example, Miss Elizabeth Craig's *Wine, Woman and a Saucepan* and Mrs Vandyke Price's *Cooking with Wine*) which will show you how to make gourmet's dishes by the use of the ends of coarse or unsatisfactory bottles of sherry, port, burgundy, claret, Graves, madeira – everything, in fact, except Quinine Wine.

Secondly: if you think it a waste to use poor wines for cooking (you are mistaken if you do) there is still a way of drinking them. All but the nastiest of wines can be used either for hot spiced wine or for cups. Hot wine, usually called punch, is best made with indifferent red wine. There are many recipes, and you will before long invent your own, but like the *Kama-Sutra* they are all elegant variations upon one primary combination. The fundamental hot *punch* consists of a bottle of coarse red wine, to which is added an orange and, if you like it, a lemon, cut in very thin rings. Put in sugar to taste, a very generous pinch of mixed spices, and water according to your judgment; stir and heat, pressing the fruit, but do not boil, skim if needed, drink while hot. You can vary this by adding brandy, liqueurs (not rum or whisky) and cloves; you can set it alight and blow it out. For *cup* a third-class white wine is better: add to it all the fruits you have, cut thin, and let them soak in it a little while. Put in plenty of ice-cubes and half as much again (or more, or less, as you think wise) of soda-water. Do not forget that some melon rind, some cucumber skin, or the herb called borage, will add a brisk flavour that you will miss if it isn't there. Here, too, you must add sugar to taste, and can drop in liqueurs, port, dark sherry or Italian vermouth as you please; but, once again, not whisky or rum.

3. Wines before Food

*Effects of cocktails compared with sherry – Fino,
Amontillado, Oloroso, Amoroso; East India
brown; Manzanilla, Macharnudo, Montilla –
Soleras – The 'flor' – Sherry's resistance to air
and time – Shippers' names.*

SHERRY is the best drink before a meal. It has no dis-
advantage, except for a small number of people with
whom it genuinely disagrees (and of these about a third
have only tried bad or doctored sherry). It has no superior
except, for grand occasions, a glass of cool and dry champagne. It has no equal, although the memory halts for a
moment over a dry madeira. Boston businessmen (I am
told) of the last century used to offer callers about eleven
in the morning a glass of dry madeira and a biscuit; it
must have been a very different and more amiable city.
Perhaps, at that time and not immediately before lunch
or dinner, madeira has an advantage over sherry. *Solvitur
ambulando*; the question is one to be settled by experiment
and not by speculation.

But there is no doubt at all that sherry is infinitely
superior to cocktails, except for the one purpose of making
people drunk. It takes much more sherry than it does cocktails to make a woman or man noisy and silly; indeed,
most people will never on sherry reach the levels of foolish-
ness to which a series of strong cocktails will carry them.
For after a few glasses of sherry your mouth and stomach

begin to remonstrate with you, and tell you that some solid food is now needed. But cocktails draw you on; there is always a reason for just one more, for you have paralysed the natural signals of danger.

A cocktail does two opposing things, both unwise. It sends down the equivalent of a violent stimulant to the stomach, in the form of a shot of spirits (usually crude, for why waste good brandy or rum where its taste is hidden?); at the same time it numbs it with the ice which alone makes the thing drinkable. With one blow it flogs it forward; with another it stuns it. So far from preparing the body for food, which is the usual defence, a cocktail does the reverse. Watch and listen to any group of people who have had plenty of cocktails sitting down to table; you can tell at once that they won't know what they're eating, and they won't care. Their stomachs are in a turmoil, and so are their voices and their heads.

Of all apéritifs, even of sherry, it is unwise to take much without some solid food. An olive, a biscuit, a cheese-straw – a scrap of something makes a great deal of difference; and the meal itself should not be too long in following. For alcohol stimulates the gastric juices, and it is not sensible to rouse them and give them nothing to do. They should not be left rushing round the walls of your stomach, seeking what they may devour. That is one of the many ways of setting up ulcers.

Sherry takes its name from the Spanish town of Jerez de la Frontera (pronounced *Herreth* and sometimes still spelt Xeres).

It is probably the descendant, but not the only descendant, of the Elizabethan 'sack'; some of that certainly came from the Canaries. (Canary sack still exists, but there is not much of it; its taste is practically indistinguishable from a medium sherry.) Most, though not quite all, sherries come from Jerez, and early on in their career they are divided, or divide themselves, into two main categories. There will afterwards be subdivisions, but initially the question a sherry maker has to answer – using his nose rather than his tongue – is: 'Will this wine be a *Fino* or an *Oloroso*?' In simpler phraseology: will it be a dry sherry or a full sherry? There is a probability that certain vineyards will produce Finos and others Olorosos, but there is no certainty, and no decision can be made until six months after the vintage. After it is made, the casks are marked with chalk marks called 'rayas'. The most usual marking is one raya for the best wine, two for the second grade wine, three for the third grade, and a grill of four for wine only worth distilling; but this marking is not universal; there are others; as for example a split stroke called a 'palo', used to indicate a Fino, or a crossed O, like a theta, to indicate an Oloroso. Nearly all sherry is made from the Palomino grape; the Pedro Ximenes grape makes a sweet and strong liquid which is added to the fuller wines or occasionally drunk by itself, almost as a liqueur.

The chief subdivision of the Finos is the *Amontillados*. The pure Fino tends to be extremely dry, and to be more popular in Spain than abroad; the Amontillado is slightly fuller, and less dry. Both wines are pale and dry, with the very individual sherry taste which is inadequately called 'nutty'. Like all other sherries, they are fortified. *Palo Cortado*, a rather rare name now, indicates a wine midway between a Fino and an Amontillado. *Vino de Pasto* just means the equivalent of 'table wine' and is no especial guide. The *Olorosos* are the wines which are called 'golden sherries' 'Bristol Milks' and so forth; Amoroso is a rich sort of Oloroso. They are sweet, and darker – in fact, conventionally, the darkness of a sherry is regarded as a clue to its sweetness. The darkest of all is also the sweetest, the so-called *East India Brown*, which owes its name to a belief held last century, and not necessarily untrue, that these heavy fortified and sweetened wines were improved by being sent out in cask to India and back again. It is really a dessert wine like port, and it would be odd to drink it as an apéritif.

There are also common names which are those of districts as well as types. *Manzanilla* is a very dry, very pale wine whose taste is very delicate and very easy to destroy. It should be made from the grapes grown in San Lucar de Barrameda, a town some distance from Jerez, on the sea-coast, which has the distinction of having set up in 1873 an Anarchist government. The experiment did not last long enough to show what would be the results of a government which was in principle opposed to all government; the wine, however, is also unusual. It is very dry, of the sort of sharpness which seems to dry up the roof of the mouth. Those who are accustomed to it tend to prefer it to all others; but it is an acquired taste and should not usually be served to newcomers. *Macharnudo* is a wine – usually excellent and reasonably dry – from the hillsides of that name a short distance from Jerez. The hill is chalky (*albariza*), and it is from chalky soil that all the best sherries come; the sandy soils produce coarser wines. *Montilla* comes from the province of Cordova; Amontillado originally took its name from Montilla, for the flavour is very similar. Montilla is outside the Jerez area and therefore not a *vino de Jerez*, but it is certainly a sherry.

The word 'Solera' with a date on a bottle has misled many innocent consumers. The date is not that of a vintage. 'Solera' is a word used for a butt standing on the ground; nearly all sherries are now soleras. Several butts of sherry are stacked in tiers filled with the same type of wine, blended, and always of the same blend. From the lowest, on ground level (Latin *solum*, floor), there is drawn off wine for blending – never more than half the butt – and this is refilled from the next butt, and so on, up to the top, which is refilled from new wine of the proper category. Each level of butts is called a *criadera;* the more *criaderas* there are, the finer the wine. The date on the bottle is the date of the bottom butt; but the percentage of wine of that date may be very small. No other wine, bar madeira, is treated in this way. Another peculiarity of sherry is that it is fermented, not in cellars and protected from the air, but in loosely bunged casks above ground. Within it forms a filmy growth called the 'flower' (*flor*) which spreads throughout the Finos and Amontillados, and sometimes also in Olorosos. It is believed that this is what gives to dry sherries their individual taste.

For this or another reason, sherry in its after years has immense powers of resistance to the air, and even to noxious vapours. It can be tasted even through a cloud of cigarette smoke. Any other wine when decanted immediately begins to change and in a few hours the air will draw from it most of its character. Not so sherry, except the lightest Finos; almost any fuller sherry actually improves in decanter. It will stay, not indeed for ever, but for many days undamaged; and on the second day it is often better than on the first. Moreover, sherry and madeira are the only two wines which are of endless age. Their term of life is undiscovered. Burgundy will die in a quarter of a century, and port in half a century; it is not known when, if ever, properly bottled and corked sherry and madeira will cease to be good. I have myself drunk an Oloroso laid down in 1780 by the original William Garvey; it was very dark, alcoholic, and with a curious concentrated taste; but it was still undoubtedly an authentic sherry.

Effectively, there are no vintage years nowadays; just occasionally a few wines are set aside, which are called *añadas*. Since therefore the merit of a sherry lies in blending, the purchaser naturally looks on the bottles for the names of the shippers (who mostly but not always have their own *bodegas* or wine lodges). There are many, and most of them nowadays very reliable. Speaking merely from my own experience, I note Pedro Domecq as offering steadily high quality wines; Garvey for a very remarkable Fino (San Patricio); Sandeman for Olorosos; Diestro for Manzanilla; Avery for a very fine range; and Williams & Humbert for never failing to reach the standard I expected. Particular wines which have always been reliable are: (very dry) San Patricio, Dos Cortados, Elizabetha, La Ina, and Pando; (rich) Bristol Milk.

(ii) OTHER SHERRIES

Treatment of indifferent sherries – Cape sherries – Australians.

'SHERRY' by itself means Spanish sherry; to offer other wines under that name alone is dishonest. But there are other wines of the same type, and 'sherry' is an English, not a Spanish word. They are now, by usage, entitled to call themselves 'South African', 'Australian', or 'Californian' sherries, so long as they retain the adjective.

Most of them do not deserve more than a casual mention; their only merit is that they are cheap. They are often only pretty poor white wines, sugared, fortified, coloured, and doctored into some resemblance to sherry. Palestinian sherry could be, and some day will be, good if rather rich; but at present it is drunk outside that country mostly out of loyalty. Cyprus sherry is a bit but not much

56

better. British sherry is made in England out of (one presumes) imported must; it rarely has any taste.

There are many occasions when a man will have to cope with the lesser sherries. Either his host is a man with little taste – a whisky-drinker or even a water-drinker – whom he does not wish to offend, or he may himself be hard up, and unable to afford anything better. If he lands a poor one, let me suggest he puts with it a touch of bitters. 'Sherry and bitters' was a common Victorian drink, because Victorian sherry was often very poor stuff. It will not give him the taste of sherry, but it will remove the dull flatness of the wine; and it is certainly better than wounding his stomach with half-frozen gin and synthetic orange juice.

Of non-Spanish sherries one group, the Cape sherries, is the most popular; they are usually, and honestly, called South African on the bottles, but there are no wines worth considering produced outside the Cape province. Their quality arises partly at least from their antiquity. Johann van Riebeeck planted the first vines as long ago as 1658. The natural wines of the Cape are, with certain exceptions noticed elsewhere, not distinguished. But distinction in sherries is acquired anyhow by blending; art or skill has provided for the Cape sherries what the natural wines may have lacked. There are now available a great many low-priced and palatable wines ranging from very dry to full. They are not usually described in detail, and their labels contain nothing more informative than 'Best South African Sherry: Medium Dry,' or some such phrases. One bottle may be excellent and the next indifferent; the customer has to rely blindly upon the judgment of his wine-merchant. I have found pretty regularly reliable, however, a very dry Cape sherry named Sterredroom, and another called Indaaba; there is also a satisfactory series called Mymering, Renasans, Onzerust and Voortrekker, in ascending degrees of sweetness. The Australians have gone to great trouble with their sherries, and have cultivated 'flors' imported from Spain with great care. Some flors that they have produced are great successes; and the wines so produced are certainly superior to any Cape sherries. However, until the Australians impose upon their exporters something like the discipline of the South Africans, and hold back some of the truly deplorable sweet wines which call themselves imperial sherries, they will not have the reputation that they could have; meanwhile, the best rule in choosing Australian sherry is to look for the word 'flor' on the label, and to choose, among those which have it, a dry in preference to a medium. The brands called Mildara, Seppelts' Dry Solero Flor, Dryad, and Chiquita are to be recommended, among those which are easily found in Britain.

(iii) THE FRENCH APÉRITIFS

Vermouths – Quinine Wines –
Bitter-Sweets – Pastis and Absinthes – The best apéritifs.

THERE is a class of wines which are rarely listed and which yet are drunk in taverns more – I suppose – than any others, at least by tourists in France. The hoardings are covered with exhortations to drink them: 'Buvez un Clacquesin! Du Beau, Du Bon, Dubonnet! Pernod, le seul veritable! Rossi – exigez la Marque!' Perhaps the wise man would ignore them, but it is impossible wholly to resist the clamour; and it is an attractive motto to try anything once. Here, then, is a brief guide.

The best of these wines are the vermouths. None of these are natural wines; all are concocted, but the vermouths are nearer to genuine wines than the others, and it is possible to speak of good and bad brands among them. The 'French' is paler than the typical 'Italian'; it has more of the original taste of white wine and herbs, and is less sweet. Nor does it have the marked bark-like or leathery taste which is typical of the Italian type. The best French Vermouth is Chambéry, then Noilly Prat; there is not much difference among the Italians, Martini is the best known; this firm, Cinzano and Gancia sell a white vermouth which is very sweet and needs to be very cold. All of these, being made-up wines, can be and are imitated in Australia, Great Britain, South Africa and the United States; the imitations are often successful. The two types can be served mixed, or by themselves, with soda, or with gin. The French goes well with cassis (black currant liqueur or syrup). Like all apéritifs they should be taken cold, and it is impossible to claim that their quality is such that ice does them harm. A sliver of lemon brightens up the Italian; 'Rossi' contains this tang already in the bottle.

The next family of drinks is the 'Quinas'. These are sweet fortified wines flavoured with quinine. Dubonnet is the most famous. St Raphael is slightly sweeter, Byrrh and Lillet slightly sharper, Bonal has also a flavouring of gentian. In all of these the quinine masks the sweetness so that they do not appear to be sickly; still, they cloy fairly soon. No matter what the French advertisements say, they have no medical use; but they are not harmful. Very similar to them is the drink called Cap Corse, in which the vanilla taste predominates.

The next most advertised group is the bitter drinks. The most distinctive is the gentian-flavoured Suze; it is very dry, bright yellow, and has a low alcoholic content. Amer Picon is dark brown and very bitter; except for addicts it is more palatable with grenadine or some other syrup added. Clacquesin is even bitterer and there is the horrible drink called Fernet Branca, whose real function is to pull you together with a violent jar after an alcoholic excess the night before. Cousins of the bitters are the bitter-sweets. Mostly, they are dark brown, sharp but with a secondary sweet tang of orange or tangerine. The best-known are Campari, Punt e Mes, Féze and Mandarin. The last is frequently drunk with curaçao, which makes a mild but certain purgative. With all these, soda-water and ice are mixed, and often a slice of citrus fruit is added.

Soda-water should never be mixed with the most popular and violent apéritifs, which are generically called 'pastis' or 'anis'. They are made by secret processes and are generally green (but the Greek equivalent, ouzo, is white and some Provençal home-made pastis is orange). When in bottle they are clear, but as soon as water is put with them they become cloudy. They taste of aniseed, and until you are used to them they have a violently stimulating effect. They are among the most questionable and habit-forming drinks known to man, and in their strongest forms are forbidden even in France. In their original strengths they were called absinthes, and contained wormwood, which is provably a deleterious substance. The brands sold in France have 45 degrees, usually, of alcohol; the brands sold in Belgium and Spain have 68 degrees or more. The best established is Pernod (note that there is more than one house of this name); the next most popular are Berger, Ricard, Pec, and Duval.

There is a pleasant, not very distinctive drink called Pineau which is made from grape-juice and brandy in Charente (where cognac comes from) and served in quantities in railway trains. But the best apéritif for a traveller in France is none of these things, but any young white burgundy with a dash of cassis liqueur in it. If this is too expensive, he should take its proletarian equivalent, a 'vin rouge-grenadine' or a 'vin blanc-citron', a red wine with grenadine or a white wine with lemon syrup. If he is with a Frenchman he can offer him 'un porto' which is like a cold and thin port. But he should not drink it himself.

4. Claret, Burgundy and other French Wines

(i) CLARET OR BORDEAUX

Soils that produce good wines – 'Bordeaux' and subdivisions explained – Médoc and Haut-Médoc The 1855 classifications – Graves – Sauternes – Côtes de Bordeaux, Entre-deux-Mers, etc. – Co-operatives – St Emilion, Pomerol – Other Bordeaux wines – List of 'bourgeois' wines – How long to keep clarets.

IN this chapter will be found no account of Champagne or Alsatian wine. Champagne will be dealt with in the chapter on sparkling wine; Alsatians in the chapter on Rhenish. That last is not intended as a challenge to French patriotism, or as a suggestion that Alsace and Lorraine are 'really German'; it is merely because the wines are, geographically and gustatorily, a part of the great basin of the Rhine whose products have a common character and should logically be considered together.

Of the remaining vineyards of France, those of Bordeaux must come first – indeed, not only in France but in the world. Other vineyards have quality; there is nothing more lovely in their way than a superb burgundy or a first-rate hock. Other vineyards have quantity: the North African production is, or anyway, has been, staggering. But nowhere else is there both quality and quantity together; nowhere else is there so much wine and such good wine, and that is after all the ideal. The disastrous winter of 1955-56, when the cold split centenarian olive

62

trees down their centres, killed a terrifying number of Bordeaux vines, especially the older plants which give distinction to the wine in bottle. Production and quality fell, and were only recovering in the sixties (for a newly-planted vine should never be cropped in its first three years, and it is better to leave it for five years). The economical wine buyer, therefore, was forced to turn to other areas and even other countries. But though the Bordeaux district will probably never recover its overwhelming primacy in that market, it is and will remain the best and most plentiful source of good red table wines in the world.

Wherever fine wines are produced the soil is poor and difficult. In the Gironde it is grey, light, shallow, dusty, stony or dry – often all six. Some of the most famous clarets come from stunted vines on land where a carrot would not grow. Left to themselves, the fields would support heather, thistles, and a little clover; before the vines came they generally did. Not that the Gironde is an ugly or dreary country. Its flat or gently rolling lands are dotted with châteaux, frequently seventeenth- and eighteenth-century manor houses with beautifully proportioned rooms, and among them are such earlier treasures as Château d'Yquem in Sauternes, with its twelfth-century towers greyly dominating the green plain. Bordeaux itself is a handsome city, with a famous long stone bridge crossing the great river Garonne. The vineyards come right up to its edge: the famous Haut-Brion and La Mission Haut-Brion are actually in the town. St Emilion is a tiny town with thirteenth-century walls, ruined cloisters, and an astonishing ancient church hollowed out of the living rock.

The district under vines delimited as 'Bordeaux' is so large that it is subdivided three times over. (The map printed as a frontispiece to this book will make what follows clearer.) The area as a whole is called 'Bordeaux';

a wine so labelled merely claims to come from, or be blended of wines from, that area. It will be an ordinary wine, but better than most which do not bear that label. More character can be expected of a wine which has the label of a region within the Bordeaux area – Médoc, Haut-Médoc, Graves, Sauternes, Entre-deux-Mers, St Emilion, Pomerol, Bourg, Blaye, or some smaller areas. These wines will show certain differences of taste already, but are unlikely to be more than satisfactory table wines for drinking freely. Within the region, however, is the Commune, such as St Estèphe or St Julien; at this point the individual characters become very marked, and one of the pleasures of claret-drinking is to note and savour the difference of taste between, say, a Margaux and a St Estèphe, though only a few miles separate the two places. Within the Commune, finally, is the Château itself (which may be no more than a farmhouse) whose proprietor thinks, or hopes, that his wine is unique. The wine may be made exclusively from a very small area, one or two fields, and what makes it exceptionally good – or indifferent – is unknown. A field which produces a 'grand cru' famous across the world may be separated by no more than a footpath from one to all appearances exactly similar in soil, site, and drainage which produces nothing but a purple peasant ordinaire. The label on a bottle, thus, may indicate as many as four degrees of classification, the first being the narrowest, as, to take an imaginary example:

CHÂTEAU VAZYVOIRE-SUR-LACARTE
SAINT-SEURIN DE CADOURNE
HAUT-MEDOC
GRAND VIN DE BORDEAUX.

These divisions, the vineyards, and the methods of viticulture allowed are laid down in detail by French law; inaccurate descriptions should have disappeared since the appearance of L. Larmat's officially authorized *Atlas de La France Vinicole* (on which what follows is based), but they haven't.

The first great division within the Bordeaux area, starting at the end of the estuary, on the west side, is the Médoc, consisting of the area north of the rivulet called the Blanquefort. It is an area of red wines: among its hundreds of châteaux there are only nineteen listed as making white wines, and only two of these (La Dame Blanche and Pavillon Blanc de Margaux) have much reputation abroad. Their flavour is like Graves, which will be spoken of later. The Médoc is divided into the lower Médoc to the north, and the Haut-Médoc to the south. The lower Médoc, which on bottle labels appears simply as 'Médoc', contains few famous wines, though Châteaux Laujac and Loudenne are deservedly well-liked in Britain, and others ought to be. But the Haut-Médoc is studded with great names. The best-known of Haut-Médoc communes are: Margaux, Pauillac, St Estèphe, St Julien, Moulis and Listrac. Cantenac is nowadays usually included in Margaux. Next would come Cissac, Cussac, Ludon, Macau, St Laurent, St Seurin-de-Cadourne, Soussans and Vertheuil. The remaining places authentically in Haut-Médoc are: Arcins, Arsac, Avensan, Blanquefort, Castelnau, Labarde, Lamarque, Le-Plan-Médoc, Le Taillan, Parempuyre, St Aubin, St Médard, St Sauveur. Good wines come from all of them. The practice of adding sugar or syrup to the wine in bad years, called 'chaptalization', is forbidden in the Bordeaux area unless a special official authorization is given, as it often is. This is one reason why clarets are claimed to be the purest and most natural of all red wines.

In the year 1855 a classification was made of the red wines of the Médoc; as it is still the only classification it had better be reprinted here:

1ers Crus

Château Lafite	Pauillac
Château Margaux	Margaux
Château Latour	Pauillac
Château Mouton Rothschild*	,,

2es Crus

Château Brane-Cantenac	Cantenac
Château Cos-d'Estournel	Saint-Estèphe
Château Montrose	,, ,,
Château Ducru-Beaucaillou	Saint-Julien
Château Gruaud-Larose	,, ,,
Château Leoville-Lascases	,, ,,
Château Leoville-Poyferré	,, ,,
Château Leoville-Barton	,, ,,
Château Lascombes	Margaux
Château Rauzan-Ségla	,,
Château Rauzan-Gassies	,,
Château Pichon-Longueville-Lalande	Pauillac
Château Pichon-Longueville	,,

3es Crus

Château Kirwan	Cantenac
Château Calon-Segur	Saint-Estèphe
Château Cantenac-Brown	Cantenac
Château d'Issan	,,
Château Palmer	Margaux
Château Desmirail	,,
Château Ferrière	,,

* Elevated from 2me cru in 1973.

Château Malescot-Saint-Exupéry	Margaux
Château Marquis-d'Alesme-Becker	,,
Château Giscours	Labarde
Château Lagrange	Saint-Julien
Château Langoa	,, ,,
Château La Lagune	Ludon

4es Crus

Château Beychevelle	Saint-Julien
Château Branaire-Ducru	,, ,,
Château Saint-Pierre	,, ,,
Château Talbot	,, ,,
Château Duhart-Milon	Pauillac
Château La Tour-Carnet	Saint-Laurent
Château Le Prieuré*	Cantenac
Château Pouget	,,
Château Marquis-de-Terme	Margaux
Château Rochet	Saint-Estèphe

5es Crus

Château Pontet-Canet	Pauillac
Château Batailley	,,
Château Croizet-Bages	,,
Château Grand-Puy-Ducasse	,,
Château Grand-Puy-Lacoste	,,
Château Haut-Bages-Libéral	,,
Château Lynch-Bages	,,
Château Lynch-Moussas	,,
Château Dauzac	Labarde
Château Mouton d'Armailhacq†	Pauillac

* Now called Prieuré-Lichine.

† Now called Mouton Baron Philippe. The wine called 'Mouton Cadet' is often sold by unscrupulous hotel-keepers at prices suggesting it is one of the two Mouton chateaux. It is not; it is a blend of Bordeaux wines made by the same firm.

Château Pédesclaux	Pauillac
Château Clerc-Milon-Mondon	,,
Château Belgrave	Saint-Laurent
Château Camensac	,, ,,
Château Cantemerle	Macau
Château Cos-Labory	Saint-Estèphe
Château du Tertre	Arsac

Crus Exceptionnels

Château Angludet	Cantenac
Château La Couronne	Pauillac
Château Bel-Air Marquis d'Aligre	Soussans
Château Chasse-Spleen	Moulis
Château Moulin-Riche	Saint-Julien
Château Poujeaux-Theil	Moulis
Château Villegeorge	Avensan

The Château Haut-Brion was commonly added to the
1er Crus – improperly, because it is a Graves and not a
Médoc.

This list is about as unsatisfactory as any list could be.
From the beginning it had a central fault; the numbers
1 to 5 were naturally supposed to be numberings by
quality, but they were not. They were a record of the prices
fetched by the various wines shortly before 1855 and a
'5th cru classé' was not a fifth-rate wine necessarily; it
might merely have been lighter, or more plentiful, than
the others. Moreover, it is more than a century out of
date. Of the four 'great firsts' two (Margaux and Haut-
Brion) have passed through periods in which they have
been widely criticised, while for years everyone agreed that
Mouton Rothschild ought to be among the firsts: it now
is. Others also, such as Pontet Canet, Beychevelle or
Chasse-Spleen, should long ago have been promoted.

When the St Emilion wines, a decade ago, acquired a classification and therefore other wines than the Médocains could officially call themselves 'Premiers Crus Classés' the Médoc proprietors were shocked out of their complacency, and serious endeavours were made to agree on a revised list. But, up till now, vested industries and jealousies have prevented any agreement; the Gordian knot was not even cut by a newcomer, Mr Lichine, who bought the Château Prieuré, and blandly issued a new list of his own. Mouton apart, the old list stands, and the best one can say is that no wine on it lacks the individual claret flavour. In buying them, a purchaser is assured of at least a minimum standard of quality; but he should be certain that he is buying what he thinks he is. 'Château Lafite' for example, is so spelt; there are plenty of Châteaux Lafitte-Machin, Moron-Lafitte, and so forth which are not the great wine at all, but have been purchased by the innocent before now.

Below the Crus Classés, however, are some hundreds of good wines called 'bourgeois'. Since the Crus on the list are generally overpriced just because they are on it, these bourgeois wines are often wiser purchases for those who have to watch their purses, both in Médoc wines and elsewhere. I shall speak about them later.

Southwards from the Médoc the next great region is GRAVES. It circles round the city of Bordeaux, runs south along the banks of the Garonne until just west of the village of Castillon; the districts of Cérons and Sauternes are enclaves within it. 'Graves' in Britain and the United States usually is thought to mean a sweet white wine; but that is no more than a half-truth. More red than white wine is made in this area, and a good – and increasing – proportion even of the white wine is dry. But much more white than red is exported, and if the purchasers of Graves abroad expect it to be sweet, sweet it generally is. This perversion of fact to suit the consumer offers an advantage to the intelligent buyer; he is likely to get a red Graves cheaper than he should. Many of the well-known châteaux in Graves produce both red and white wines.

In 1953 a Graves Classification (revised in 1959) was issued of the best vineyards, in alphabetical order, for 'Classified' red-and-white, red, and white wines:

Vineyards making red and white wine

Château Bouscaut	Cadaujac
Château Carbonnieur	Léognan
Domaine de Chevalier	Léognan
Château Haut-Brion	Pessac
Château La Tour-Martillac	Martillac
Château Malartic-Lagravière	Léognan
Château Olivier	Léognan

Vineyards making red wine

Château de Fieuzal	Léognan
Château Haut-Bailly	Léognan
Château La Mission-Haut-Brion	Pessac
Château La Tour-Haut-Brion	Talence
Château Pape-Clément	Pessac
Château Smith-Haut-Lafitte	Martillac

Vineyards making white wine

Château Couhins	Villenave-d'Ornan
Château Laville-Haut-Brion	Talence

The two enclaves in Graves already mentioned, Cérons and Sauternes, produce the full sweet wines which Frenchmen drink at the end of their meals or with pâté de foie.

They are delightful wines, taken at the right time – which is after the main dish, with fruit or dessert. Fruit will take the edge off its syrupy sweetness and the palate can appreciate its perfumed flavour. Its lushness is due to the fact that the grapes are reaped when over-ripe and attacked by the mildew 'Botrytis Cinerea' ('pourriture noble', noble rot, is the official phrase, included in the laws). At one time the picked grapes were also laid out on straw in the sun to ripen yet further; the phrase 'vin de paille' (straw wine) is still sometimes used. The proportion of sugar to water is naturally much higher in over-ripe grapes, and this is reflected in the sweetness of the wine, but the floweriness of the flavour is due to the corruption.

Facing Sauternes and Cérons, across the River Garonne, are the two small areas of LOUPIAC and STE-CROIX-DU-MONT, which produce very similar wines, though in smaller quantities and with no famous names. CÉRONS includes three communes – Cérons, Illats, and Podensac – and its wines were until lately marketed abroad under the title Graves; consequently, it may be, only the name of the Château de Cérons itself is at all well known. SAUTERNES, on the other hand, is world-famous; too world-famous, indeed, for almost any white wine of any country whose only characteristic is sickly sweetness tries to steal its name. The true Sauternes were classified, with the Médocs, in 1855, in a list which is less subject to challenge, though probably there are some wines, such as the Château Cantegril, which would be included in a revision. ('Haut Sauternes' is a phrase that has no meaning; it was only used, in the words of a French producer 'to oblige our English friends'.)

1er Cru Superieur

Château d'Yquem   Sauternes

1ers *Crus*

Château La Tour-Blanche	Bommes
Château Lafaurie-Peyraguey	,,
Clos Haut-Peyraguey	,,
Château Rayne-Vigneau	,,
Château de Suduiraut	Preignac
Château Coutet	Barsac
Château Climens	,,
Château Guiraud	Sauternes
Château Rieussec	Fargues
Château Rabaud	Bommes

2es *Crus*

Château de Myrat	Barsac
Château Doisy-Daëne	,,
Château Doisy-Vedrines	,,
Château d'Arche	Sauternes
Château d'Arche-Lafaurie	,,
Château Filhot	,,
Château Broustet	Barsac
Château Caillou	,,
Château Suau	,,
Château de Malle	Preignac
Château Romer	Fargues
Château Lamothe	Sauternes
Château Nairac	Barsac

The Communes included in Sauternes are: Sauternes itself, Preignac, Fargues, Bommes and Barsac.

Barsac is so famous in its own right that many people imagine it to be a different wine; it is however really a Sauternes. All true Sauternes must be dear, because the grapes must be left on the vines until they are almost raisiny and the crop is small; Yquem fetches absurd prices.

Recently, some of the Sauternes châteaux have tried the experiment of producing dry wines. Yquem called its one 'Ygrec'. Not all the efforts were successful; Ch. Filhot is among those that were.

Along the east side of the Garonne, opposite Graves, is a thin line of vineyards called CÔTES DE BORDEAUX. The most northerly part produces red wines, the rest white. The northern part is called 'Premières Côtes'; after it has circled round Loupiac and Ste-Croix du Mont the name is changed to 'Côtes de Bordeaux-St-Macaire'. The wines, especially the reds, are good honest wines, and are usually under-priced. There is no classification and here too the good advice is to buy the equivalent of 'bourgeois' wines. The same is true of the (mainly white) products of the great area of ENTRE-DEUX-MERS ('Between-two-waters', the waters being the Rivers Garonne and Dordogne). In both of these districts, as in the smaller adjoining areas of GRAVES-DE-VAYRES and STE-FOY-BORDEAUX, the quantity and quality of the wine has been greatly improved in the last twenty years by the co-operatives. The small peasant proprietor could not be relied upon in the past to produce regularly a wine up to the standard; and a few incompetent *vignerons* were enough to ruin the name of a whole parish. The great *caves co-opératives* (which now take the majority of the wine in the largest area, Entre-deux-mers), levelled up the worst producers by declining to accept grapes below a certain standard, and by pressing and fermenting what they accepted in the most modern vats and by the latest machinery. Wine so made can never be a great wine, for blending on such a large scale destroys individual character. But the wine made by the co-operatives is good wine; even in the aristocratic Haut-Médoc there are several co-operatives whose effect on the quality of the 'small wines' has been admirable.

73

Swinging round north, and crossing the Dordogne, we come to the last of the great wine-producing areas of Bordeaux, SAINT EMILION and its dependencies. There are 160 châteaux listed in the Commune of St Emilion itself, and one and a half times as many in the surrounding communes. Of these, the districts of Lussac, Montagne, Parsac, Puisseguin, and St-Georges are allowed to attach the name 'St Emilion' to their labels; as was Sables until quite recently. The wines produced in the nearby area of NEAC are very similar to the St Emilionnais. But there are few great names in Néac or the hyphened Communes; the famous wines come from St Emilion proper, between the brook Barbanne and the river Dordogne. In this charming little thirteenth-century town there exists an institution which has no exact parallel in France. The Médocain and Burgundian societies – the Compagnons du Bon Temps and the Chevaliers de Tastevin – which seem similar are, in fact, recent sociable and publicity-seeking bodies; the Jurade de St Emilion is in fact as well as form a survival from an earlier age. Most of its powers, if not formerly repealed, are obsolete, but it still declares whether or no a vintage deserves to be labelled 'St Emilion', and it gives or withholds its Seal to the wines of individual châteaux after tasting them. It was founded in the reign of Richard Coeur de Lion, and its first charter dates from 1199, granted by King John of England. During the late 19th century it was dormant, but there is a continuous line of 'Premiers Jurats' from the Middle Ages till today.

All St Emilions are fuller than Médoc wines; they are midway between the other clarets and the burgundies. They have the reputation of being powerful wines; when King Louis XIII was forced to stay here for many months his courtiers (says the historian of Libourne) drank so much of them that *plusieurs en moururent et davantage en naquirent*. They are all reds, they have a splendid bouquet and plenty of body. But beyond that there comes a marked distinction between the wines of the hill and the plain. St Emilion town sits upon a limestone outcrop, on which there is but a shallow soil. The famous 'monolithic' church of St Emilion was hollowed out of this rock, and when the need of a spire was felt, it had to be built above it, forcing its way through the village square and soaring up into the sky. A man can lean against the church spire halfway up, like Baron Munchausen's horse. The wines made on this hill are powerful, with a very strong and individual bouquet. The most famous name here is the Château Ausone, first planted, they say, by the Roman poet Ausonius. Round the hill, in the low-lying fields, are vineyards producing wines which are less powerful, though they have plenty of what the French call *sève* ('sap'), and are more delicate and gentle. They are full in taste and scent, but require less time to develop; five years is often enough. The most famous name here is Cheval Blanc; and it is the wine I should choose (if I had to make so preposterous a choice) as the wine that I have liked best of all French wines.

An official classification of St Emilion wines was made in 1955. It is not out of date, like the Médoc list, but it has been challenged as too comprehensive. It is due for revision every ten years; meanwhile, here it is:

Premier Grand Cru Classé:
   (A) Châteaux *Ausone; †Cheval Blanc.
   (B) Châteaux Beauséjour (Duffau Lagarrosse);
   *Beauséjour (Bécot); *Belair; *Canon; *Clos Fourtet;
   †Figeac; *La Gaffelière; *Magdelaine; Pavie;
   *Trottevielle.

Grand Cru Classé:

L'Angélus; L'Arrosée; Baleau; *Balestard-la-Tonnelle; Bellevue; Bergat; Cadet-Bon; Cadet-Piola; *Canon-la-Gaffelière; *Cap de Mourlin; Chapelle Madeleine; Le-Chatelet; Chauvin; Coutet; Couvent-des-Jacobins; †Croque-Michotte; *Curé-Bon; Dassault; Faurie-de-Souchard; Fonplégade; Fonroque; †Franc-Mayne; Grand-Barrail-Lamarzelle-Figeac; Grand-Corbin; †Grand Corbin-Despagne; †Grand-Mayne; †Grand-Pontet; Grandes-Murailles; Guadet-St.-Julien; Haut-Corbin; *Clos des Jacobins; Jean Faure; La Carte; *La Clotte; La Cluzière; La Couspaude; La Dominique; Clos la Madeleine; La Marzelle; La Tour-Figeac; La Tour-du-Pin-Figeac; Laniotte; Chapelle-de-la-Trinité; *Larcis-Ducasse; Larmande; Laroze; Lasserre; Le Couvent; Le Prieuré; Matras; Mauvezin; Moulin du Cadet; L'Oratoire; Pavie-Decesse; Pavie-Macquin; Pavillon-Cadet; Petit-Faurie-de-Souchard; †Ripeau; St.-Georges-Côte-Pavie; Clos St.-Martin; Sansonnet; *Soutard; Tertre-Daugay; Trimoulet; Trois-Moulins; Troplong-Mondot; *Villemaurine; †Yon-Figeac.

The order is alphabetical. I have marked with * those Hill wines which I have personally liked, and with † similar Plain wines. To the latter I would add Château Monbousquet, and remark on the consistently good standard of the St Emilion Co-operative's wine, sold as 'St Emilion Royal'.

Further to the north is the small district of POMEROL, producing not very many wines but nearly all of high quality, and, like St Emilion, practically all reds. They are very similar to the wines of St Emilion plain, perhaps

slightly less strong and heavy, as are also the wines of
LALANDE DE POMEROL, a rather unproductive region to
their north. As there is no classification of Pomerols, I will
offer a personal list of wines which I have myself enjoyed,
knowing that I must unwittingly omit some excellent
wines:

> Château Pétrus (outstanding)
> Château Beauregard
> Château Bourgneuf
> Château Certan-Guiraud
> Château Clinet
> Château La Conseillante
> Château Croix de Gay
> Château L'Evangile
> Château Le Gay
> Château Lafleur-Pétrus
> Château Gazin
> Château Mazeyres
> Château Nénin
> Château Petit Village
> Château Plince
> Château La Pointe
> Château Rouget
> Château Trotanoy
> Vieux Château Certan

Beyond Pomerol, northwards along first the banks of
the Dordogne and then of the Gironde are the small areas
of CÔTES DE FRONSAC and CÔTES CANON-FRONSAC and a
considerable group of honest red wines which are usually
marketed simply as BORDEAUX SUPERIEURES; still further
north are the quite reliable wines of BOURG and of BLAYE.
There is a great deal of good wine made in these areas,

but there is not much great wine. The reds far outnumber the whites. There is no classification.

Throughout this chapter I have been advising purchasers to break away from the classifications and search for the second rank, unclassified, or 'bourgeois' wines, if they want to get the best value for their money. This advice is continually repeated in all the more intelligent articles on wine in the magazines. But there are literally hundreds of such wines in Bordeaux, and no guide whatever to them is offered to the bemused purchaser anywhere that I know of. Therefore, at the risk of being charged with arrogance, I am printing here a short list of my own of about a hundred 'bourgeois' wines and their equivalents which from my own tasting I know to be good. There are many others of course which despite a resolute attention to duty I have not succeeded in tasting, or at any rate tasting sufficiently often to be sure that I should include them. I have not included the Pomerols, because I have just given my personal list, and there are few St Emilions because the official classification has already thrown its net very wide. 'M' means Médoc (upper or lower), 'G' Graves, 'P' Premières Côtes, 'F' Fronsac, 'S.E.' St Emilion, and 'B' Bourg, Blaye or Bordeaux generally. 'W' means that the product is mainly or exclusively white wine. I have not specially mentioned the co-operatives, so I will say here at the beginning that I have never found a bad wine produced by a Bordeaux co-operative (and never a great one either).

A LIST OF THE BEST UNCLASSIFIED BORDEAUX WINES

l'Abbé Gorsse de Gorsse (M)   d'Arcins (M)
d'Anseillan (M)   de Barbe (B)
d'Arche (M)   la Barde (S.E.)

du Barrail (M)
le Barrail (B)
Bellegrave (M)
Bel Orme Tronquoy de
  Lalande (M)
le Boscq (M)
Bouqueyran (M)
Bouscaut, W (G)
de la Brède (G)
Brun (S.E.)
de By (M)
Canon (F)
Canteloup (M)
Capbern (M)
de Carles (F)
Carruel (B)
la Chabanne (P)
Cheval Noir (S.E.)
Cissac (M)
Citran (M)
Clarke (M)
Closerie Grand Poujeaux (M)
Colombier Monpelou (M)
Constant Bages Monpelou
  (M)
Couhins, W (G)
Croute Charlus (B)
Domaine de Chevalier (G)
Domaine de Christoly (B)
Dutruch Grand Poujeaux (M)
Eyquem (B)
de Ferrand (S.E.)
Fonbadet (M)
Fonbelleau (P)

Fonreaud (M)
Fourcas Dupré (M)
Fourcas Hostein (M)
Franc Pourret (S.E.)
Gassies (P)
du Glana (M)
Gloria (M)
Gontier (B)
Grand St Julien (M)
Grand St Lambert (M)
La Gravette (B)
Gressier Grand Poujeaux
  (M)
Guionne (B)
Haut Bages Monpelou
  (M)
Hanteillan, W (M)
La Haye (M)
Jeandeman (F)
Labégorce (M)
Ladouys (M)
Lafleur Milon (M)
Lafon (M)
Lanessan (M)
Langlade (S.E.)
Larchevesque (F)
Larose Capbern (M)
Latour Camblanes (P)
Latour Haut Brion (G)
Latour Marbuzet (M)
Latour Martillac (G)
Latour du Mirail (M)
Latour Montagne (S.E.)
Latour de Pez (M)

Latour Puyblanquet (S.E.)
Laujac (M)
Laville Haut-Brion, W (G)
Leon (P)
Lestage (M)
Liversan (M)
Livran (M)
Loudenne (M)
Lugagnac, W (B)
du Lyonnet (S.E.)
MacCarthy (M)
Malbec (P)
Marbuzet (M)
Maucaillou (M)
Mayne Gazin (B)
Mendoce (B)
Meyney (M)
Mille Secousses (B)
Monbousquet (S.E.)
Morillon (B)
Moron Lafitte (W)
des Ormes (M)
Parempuyre (M)
Paveil de Luze (M)
Péconnet (P)
Peyrat (M)
du Peyrat (P)
de Pez (M)

Phélan Segur (M)
Pibran (M)
Pierre Bibian (M)
Pique-Caillou (G)
Pommarède (G)
Pomys (M)
de Portets (G)
Potensac (M)
Robert (B)
Le Roc (B)
Le Roq (M)
Roquegrave, W (M)
Roqueys (P)
Rosemont (M)
Rouet (F)
St Christophe (M)
St Georges (S.E.)
St Saturnin (M)
Sénéjac (M)
Siran (M)
Sociando (M)
de Terrefort (B)
La Tour de By (M)
La Tour de Mons (M)
Tuillac (B)
Tourteau Chollet, W (G)
Valrose (B)
Virelade (G)
Vray Canon Bodet (F)

How long should Bordeaux wines be kept to bring them to their finest?

The following table was printed soon after the last world war ended in a pamphlet issued by the interprofessional

Committee of the Bordeaux wine trade (C.I.V.B.):

Red Wines		Average Years	Great Vintages
Haut-Médoc:	Margaux	5 years	8 years
	St Julien	5 ,,	8 ,,
	Moulis	7 ,,	9 ,,
	Pauillac	8 ,,	10 ,,
	St Estèphe	8 ,,	10 ,,
Graves		6 ,,	8 ,,
Pomerol		6 ,,	8 ,,
St Emilion (hill wines)		8 ,,	10 ,,
St Emilion (plain wines)		6 ,,	8 ,,

But rapid changes in methods of wine-making were made almost from the moment that the Nazi régime was crushed. These changes had as their effect, and presumably as their aim, to hasten the maturing of wine, for the world's cellars were empty; 1945 was the last vintage to be handled universally in the old way. That table, therefore, may well give too long periods; in any case, as I have said already, it is better to drink a wine too soon than too late.

Wine is good drinking from the cask too, when it is ready for bottling, though it is different from a bottled wine – fresher and cruder. But once it is bottled, red wine becomes momentarily undrinkable. It receives a jar which produces a rather nauseating taste called 'bottle-sickness'. This should go off in a few weeks or months, but it can last a long time in the case of wines without enough acidity.

Bordeaux white wines, on the other hand, are usually excellent from the moment of their bottling, and rarely improve after about three years. Indeed, the only noticeable change is a darkening of colour, called *madérisation*. Some people find that a 'flatness' in taste occurs at the same time; it may be so, but I doubt it.

(ii) BURGUNDY

Forged names – Shippers – Vines – Chablis – List of Côte de Nuits wines – Of Côte de Beaune wines, including Hospices de Beaune – Mâcon – Beaujolais.

THE penalty, or at least the consequence, of virtue is to be imitated. Some of the finest and most famous red wines in the world are produced upon a stony slope called the Côte d'Or, or Golden Hillside, in Burgundy, and some of them also have the misfortune to have easily remembered names. Therefore, Volnay, Pommard and Beaune are among the most frequently forged names in the world. He is a rash man who buys a bottle with nothing but one of those bare names on the label; he would be lucky, between the wars at any rate, to be served nothing worse than a Rumanian or Algerian red. Less known Burgundian names are safer: English and American tongues find it difficult to call for the excellent wines of Les Grands Echézeaux or Nuits St Georges, Cailles and embarrassing to ask for the Clos de Tart, so the better part of the sucker market is lost. The remedy of buying château-bottled wine is impracticable for burgundy: the vineyards are divided among so many small proprietors that 'domain' bottling is far rarer than château bottling in the Bordeaux area. The famous Clos Vougeot is divided up among over seventy owners, and its sixteenth-century château is only a meeting-place for an organization of burgundy-lovers called the Chevaliers de Tastevin. A drinker of burgundies must still rely on three things – the taste and honesty of his wine merchant, and the standing of the shipper, or the name of the vineyard or 'cuvée' within the commune. In Britain, though, if not in the United States, the label may nowadays be accepted as accurate.

There are a number of reliable shippers of burgundy. Among those located in Burgundy itself who are in good standing and whose labels are frequently seen abroad are: Bouchard Père et Fils, Louis Jadot, Joseph Drouhin, Chanson Père et Fils, Faiveley, Leroy, Louis Latour, Patriarche, Pierre Ponnelle; there are, of course, many others. In most of Burgundy the best wine comes from an aristocratic and small-fruiting vine called the Pinot, and the coarse heavy-fruiting Gamay is frowned upon, but so little is a vine to be relied on as a guide that in the Beaujolais the reverse is true and the proletarian Gamay produces the best wines. In shops and wine merchants there are frequently seen wines called, 'Passe-tous-grains': this word on a bottle means that both Pinot and Gamay grapes have been used in making the wine. The word 'Aligoté' similarly means that the contents are a white burgundy made from Aligoté grapes.

The difference between burgundy and claret is mainly one of taste, and as such very difficult to describe. Burgundy has been called the most 'masculine' of wines. It is fuller, sweeter and heavier. Its bouquet is stronger, or usually more forceful. Its fault, when it has one, is a distinct earthy or rooty flavour. It is a deep red – if a young burgundy is pinkish, be suspicious. It goes better with strong-tasting meats and game; the taste of claret is more easily overridden. It is not, when unadulterated, usually stronger nor more alcoholic; it is not, contrary to the expectations raised by its taste, as long-lived as good clarets are.

The vineyards of Burgundy follow the main railway line from Paris to the south coast, the old P.L.M. line – or, rather, it follows them. They are in shape like a shoulder. The line runs first south-east to Dijon, as if it were aiming at Switzerland; at that point it makes almost a full right-angled turn and goes south-south-west to

Lyons. The first stop from Paris has always been at a desolate station called Laroche-Migennes. Even many of the fastest expresses are halted there, for no reason that the traveller can see from his carriage window. The small town of modern buildings, ugly as only French provincial houses can be, and nothing else but acres of gleaming railway tracks still haunted by ghosts of wagons marked *Chevaux* 8 *Hommes* 40, and occasionally by locomotives letting out that peculiar heartbroken howl that only French engines make. It seems to be, like Bletchley in England, a halt which owes its tepid existence to some obscure railway convenience, or even to the whims of long-dead directors.

But it has purpose and excuse; it is the junction for the first of the burgundies, CHABLIS. Sometimes Chablis is said not to be a true burgundy: that is a refinement with no basis in fact. The area, as charted by the *Comité National des Appellations d'Origine des Vins et Eaux de Vie*, is clearly contained within Burgundy. (I repeat that throughout this book this committee's maps have always been followed. They are assembled in Larmat's *Atlas* and other descriptions are merely personal fantasies.) Chablis is a name which is, or was until the EEC legislation, as frequently forged as Beaune. It mayn't be forgery to describe a wine as, say, Australian Chablis; it is deplorable and shows the maker has no proper pride in his product, but the adjective 'Australian' is at least a warning. If the liquid within is of a golden colour, then it is not Chablis. Chablis is very pale yellow, almost greenish, with a quite unmistakable dry taste which makes it perhaps the pleasantest possible drink with shellfish, and almost obligatory with oysters.

As with a great many burgundies it is wise to look for the name of the vineyard as well as the district. In Chablis the best names are those of the seven grands crus, all on the slope north-east of the town of Chablis – Les Blanchots, Les Clos, Grenouilles, Bougrots, Preuses, Valmur and Vaudésir. 'Chablis-Moutonne', once the name of a registered brand, is now that of a good delimited district. A premier cru Chablis – there are 22 – is a good wine, and plain Chablis is not negligible.

No further wine of importance is produced until the traveller has passed Dijon and made his right-turn towards the south. The first vineyard then is said to be Montrecul almost in the suburbs of Dijon; I have never tasted it nor even seen its label, which should be an interesting one. But no great wines occur, nor any names likely to be seen outside France, until we are under the slopes of the hills of the Côte d'Or, starting at the Commune of Fixin (where the Clos de la Perrière is worth noting). The northerly half of the Côte is called the Côte de Nuits; the southerly the Côte de Beaune. The first is more famous for its reds, the latter for its whites; but in both there are delicious wines of both colours.

Starting from the north, the first great name in the CÔTE DE NUITS is the Commune of *Gevrey-Chambertin*. Chambertin red wines have a distinct taste of their own – so, indeed, have those of all the Communes of this Côte, but it is impossible to describe it. The Côte is Paradise for the lover of big, perfumed, heavy red wines; in that category, there is nowhere else in the world to equal it. The most remarkable vineyards in this area are: Le Chambertin, Clos de Bèze, Charmes and Latricières. The second is the only vineyard which may put the name Chambertin at the beginning of its title; the others and five more may hyphen it on. The rest have to include the word 'Gevrey'. Next is *Morey St-Denis*, where the best wines are: Clos de Tart, Clos St Denis, Clos de la Roche, Les

Lambrays, and Les Bonnes Mares. After that *Chambolle Musigny*, where I note as important Musigny, Charmes, Les Amoureuses, and the rest of Les Bonnes Mares. The last-named vineyard spreads across the two communes, and is for a Burgundian vineyard a fairly large one; at that its area is given as only about thirty-five acres. At *Vougeot*, there is, of course, the famous Clos Vougeot, since 1889 divided among over seventy small proprietors, many of them named on a great notice in his little field. So splendid was the wine from this famous Clos that during the Revolution Colonel Bisson, marching to join the army of the Rhine, halted his soldiers outside its gates and presented arms; to this day the same gesture is performed by any regiment that passes by. On the hillside, not far from the road, the old château contains the four huge wooden presses – still in working order – used by the Cistercian monks who benefited and educated humanity by planting these fields with vines. But the breaking up of their estate has not been a benefit to the wine. Some of the small proprietors make wine as fine as ever; some do not. There is a little excellent white wine produced in this Commune, from the small vineyard Clos Blanc de Vougeot.

At *Flagey-Echézeaux*, hampered by its eccentric name, there are Grands Echézeaux and Echézeaux, the first having a higher reputation. The next Commune everyone knows and most people can pronounce. *Vosne-Romanée* contains Romanée-Conti, Romanée-St Vivant, La Romanée, La Tâche, Richebourg, Malconsorts, Suchots and other less famous growths. But these great wines come from tiny fields; they must be, and are, rare. La Romanée itself is barely two acres in size. Yet they are known across the world and one of them – Richebourg – has always seemed to me the wine in which all the standard qualities of red burgundy are found in their highest degree.

It is more typical, even, than the great wine which gives its name to the whole area, *Nuits St Georges*; in that Commune note Cailles, St Georges, Vaucrains, Porrets and Boudots. With it the Côte de Nuits virtually comes to an end, for no wines of interest are produced in the remaining parishes.

The CÔTE DE BEAUNE begins with the three Communes of Pernand-Vergelesses, hampered by its names, Ladoix and *Aloxe-Corton*, of which the last is best known, and whose name is added whenever possible to the vineyards, some of which cross two or even three of them. Notable among them are Le Corton, Clos du Roi, Bressandes, Les Renardes, and Corton-Charlemagne (white). You may believe that the last-named was planted by Charlemagne if you so choose. Aux Vergelesses, another excellent wine, is generally classed in the next Commune of *Savigny*; there and in the nearby Commune of Chorey there is produced a large amount of sound wine that deserves no more enthusiastic title. It is overshadowed by the more numerous and famous wines of *Beaune* itself. Here it is more necessary than ever, with a name so frequently taken dishonestly, to look for the additional safeguard of a vineyard's name. Watch therefore for: Les Grèves, Bressandes, Cras, Cent Vignes, Les Fèves, Clos de la Mousse, Marconnets, Clos du Roi, Les Teurons, Champs Pimonts, Les Epenottes and the Clos des Mouches. Some of the wines from Les Grèves carry the name L'Enfant Jésus; I don't know why. The most famous name connected with Beaune, however, is undoubtedly the 'Hospices de Beaune'; and here some explanation is needed.

Beaune is a pretty, self-contained city. It still has its low and thick medieval walls; its narrow and bright streets are thronged with dealers in and makers of wine rather than tourists; to them, indeed, its hotels are indifferent in both senses of the word. In the middle of the city is its jewel, the 'Hôtel-Dieu' or Hospice de Beaune, a home and hospital for the aged poor, founded by the Chancellor Nicolas Rolin and his wife Guigogne de Salins in 1443 and still used for the same purpose. The Chancellor and his wife each endowed the Hospices with some of their vineyards, and ever since then pious property owners have done the same. The Hospices therefore owns vineyards scattered all over the Côte de Beaune area, and only about half of them are in Beaune itself. (They are all in the *Côte* – the others are in Aloxe-Corton, Auxey, Meursault, Monthélie, Pommard, Savigny, and Volnay.) Nevertheless, their product is all entitled to be called 'Hospices de Beaune', and is so labelled. But at the famous annual sales in the Hospice the various lots fetch very different prices, for the wine is naturally of very different quality. The highest priced are usually those from the vineyards of the founder and his wife; these always have the name 'Chancelier Rolin' or 'Guigogne de Salins' after the words Hospices de Beaune on the label. So, too, do all the better esteemed vineyards; I would be suspicious if I was confronted with a bottle labelled merely 'Hospices de Beaune'. To classify the twenty-three odd vineyards is a task for an expert, and the classification would vary each year. As no more than a personal preference, I mention, besides the two chiefs, the Dames Hospitalières, Charlotte Dumay, and a Corton called Docteur Peste after a physician whose name cannot have been his fortune.

South of Beaune are the famous and much imitated wines of *Pommard* and *Volnay*; genuine wine of either is and must be scarce. In the first, names worth looking for are Rugiens, La Platière, Argillières, Pezerolles and Epenots; reliable in the second, Caillerets, Clos des Chênes, Champans and Fremiets. At *Auxey-Duresses* and

Monthélie, nearby, wine of very similar character is produced; in these communes there are no very well-known vineyards, but for that or another reason it is not worth while to forge their names, and wines labelled merely with their names can be bought with some confidence. Immediately next to them is the town and Commune of *Meursault*, which produces, not counting Chablis, the second most famous white burgundy. Names to note are: Perrières, Charmes, Goutte d'Or, Genevrières. It could be said: 'the most famous', were it not for the next two communes of importance, *Puligny-Montrachet* and *Chassagne-Montrachet*. If the French white wines could challenge successfully the great hocks – and it is improbable that they can – it would be with the Montrachets. There is nothing to compare with them in Bordeaux. The greatest distinction in the south-west is achieved in sweet wines, of which the palate tires quickly. Nor do Bordeaux whites mature; they reach their peak in three years. The Montrachets, and to a less degree the Meursaults, provide what a wine-drinker usually misses in French white wine – a rotundity, a solidity, a sense of depth and fullness to go with its delicacy and fine bouquet. Enthusiasts debate endlessly the merits of the most famous growths: Le Montrachet, Le Chevalier Montrachet, Le Bâtard Montrachet and Bienvenu Bâtard Montrachet. For those who are unlikely to be able to afford any of them, Les Combettes, Les Pucelles, Cailleret, Clos St Jean (red) and Morgeot provide very acceptable runners-up. The last of the famous Côte d'Or wines is *Santenay*, a rather lighter, very well flavoured and perfumed wine, where the vineyard of Les Gravières is worth noting. South of the Côte d'Or, in the 'Côte Chalonnaise', there is but one wine of real distinction, *Mercurey*, which is dark coloured, and with a slight twang to it, and can be most agreeable. There are good wines, too, at Givry and Montagny (the latter solely white), some excellent white at Rully; but the next great names are MACON and BEAUJOLAIS.

These two areas perform the invaluable service of providing quantities of good red burgundy for those who cannot afford the famous growths of the Côte d'Or. Abundant, full, fragrant, and inexpensive, they lack only the final beauties of a more famous burgundy of great age; those without limitless purses and appetites should be duly grateful to them. There are few great names among the red Macons, but there is one among the whites, *Pouilly*. almost all of which is called Pouilly Fuissé. (Pouilly Vinzelles and Loché are trivial; Solutré, Chaintré and Vergisson are subdivisions of Fuissé). Just before and after the last war a great deal of thin and sourish 'Pouilly' was sold in Britain, which was partly responsible for customers shifting to another Pouilly, a long way away on the Loire. The quality of Pouilly Fuissé is now better, however. In Beaujolais, further south, the wine is almost entirely red, only a little rather dull white being produced as a sort of curiosity. Among the reds, though, there are several distinguished names. *Moulin à Vent*, in its finest years, stands level with all but the best Côte d'Or wines. Very good, too, are the wines of St Amour, Côte de Brouilly, Fleurie, Juliénas, Brouilly, Morgon, Chénas, and Chiroubles. Beaujolais is best drunk young; there are those who will drink it when it's one year old. It is lively, strong, earthy, and with a particular taste of its own. It has suffered greatly from its popularity. For the last thirty years every Paris café has had to have 'son Beaujolais', and pretty poor stuff some of it has been. The cult has spread to England and to the United States, and nowadays it is wiser, unless you know the shipper, to drink only Beaujolais which has its commune name on the bottle.

(iii) OTHER WINES

Loire wines: Vouvray, Saumur, Anjou – Rhône wines: Côte Rôtie, Hermitage, Châteauneuf du Pape, Tavel – Southern wines – Arbois – others.

THERE is only one area in France which can offer still wines comparable with claret and burgundy, and that is the basin of the great River Loire. On and near the banks of the Loire – with an 'e', feminine, and large – and its tributaries the Loir – without an 'e', masculine, and small – the Allier, the Cher and the Vienne, is produced white wine which in the Middle Ages was valued above that of Bordeaux and has been steadily coming back again into favour in recent years. There is not much red wine of interest produced here. One, though, can be found with an individual taste at Sancerre far up the river; Chinon, midway, was celebrated by Rabelais, who may well have drunk it instead of mother's milk, but is rather dull nowadays; Bourgueil nearby is a better name on a label; St Nicolas de Bourgueil better still. Anjou rosé too, from the Cabernet grape, is among the best examples of that light, lemonadey wine. But the white wines are those on which the reputation of the district rests. They are supposed to be unreliable, but more careful vintaging and marketing is removing that reproach. They are charged with being thin: in poor years (as with all northerly wines) that may be so, but it is a long way from being generally true. The 1947 Clos le Mont, a well known Vouvray, for example reached 18 degrees, a strength above nearly all table wines. They have a scented quality which is unmistakable and a tendency to sweetness without the heaviness of a Sauternes; they are commonly pale in colour. Quite a number of the wines are *pétillant*. A *pétillant* wine is a wine with a 'prickle'; the nearest description of it is 'semi-sparkling'. Carbonic acid gas is naturally produced during the fermentation of the grape; usually, it has all gone off by the time that the wine is bottled. *Pétillance* occurs when the wine in bottle is still working, and produces a non-alcoholic fermentation called 'malolactic'. Thicker bottles and stouter corks are consequently needed. While *pétillance* does not make so violent a change as the champagne process, it removes much of the bouquet, but the resultant wine is a very agreeable drink for a hot day.

Starting in the upper reaches, the first wine of importance is one that is only a 'V.D.Q.S.' and is not officially recognized as a Loire wine, but is becoming very popular and has the typical Loire character, *St Pourçain sur Sioule* high up on the Allier. (Its 1961 was remarkably good). But it is far less important than the next two groups of vineyards, *Sancerre* and *Pouilly sur Loire*, both of which have improved immensely in quality and popularity in the last decade. The Pouilly is called 'Pouilly fumé' when it is made from the grapes called 'smoky white' (*blanc fumé*). There are two well known châteaux in Pouilly, Nozet and Tracy, and the wine is charming; but it has risen so rapidly in price since it became the rival of the Burgundian Pouilly that the Sancerre, where I have noted Chavignol with particular pleasure, is usually better value. The white wine of Quincy, on the river Cher not far away, is similar; but none of these is as famous as that of *Vouvray*, a town a mile or two from Tours and the source of the finest wine of Touraine. This wine is full, with a slightly apple-like taste, and varies very greatly from vineyard to vineyard, and year to year; at its best, it is an admirable wine for drinking with fish and white meat.

Next, passing Chinon and Bourgueil already mentioned, we come to a mass of vineyards, classified as *Anjou* or *Saumur*. It is from this area that the bulk of the clean, full and inexpensive Loire whites come: if English and American buyers ever drink Loire wine on a large scale (and there are many worse things that they could do) it will be Angevin wine that they buy.

The vineyards are divided into four 'coteaux' – de l'Aubance, du Layon, de la Loire and de Saumur. In the Coteaux du Layon the Quarts de Chaume (pretty sweet) and Bonnezeaux are names to remember; in the Coteaux de la Loire, Savennières, Coulée de Serrant and Roche aux Moines; and in the Coteaux de Saumur, Turquant, Montsoreau, and Parnay, which last produces a wine of a very peculiar flavour of its own.

From there onwards to Nantes and even to the mouth of the Loire there is produced in considerable amounts a white wine called Muscadet, from the grape used in it. It has a faint, slightly musky odour; it too has risen almost too rapidly into popularity. It is as well to buy only, if you can, bottles which have 'Sèvres et Maine' or 'des Coteaux de la Loire' on the label after the word Muscadet, as they will be better than the general run of the wine. I know one good Château, Ch. de la Bidière. The fishermen of Nantes prefer to drink a coarser wine with the coarse name of Gros Plant Nantais, and save 50 centimes.

Fourth in importance among French wine-growing districts is the valley of the Rhône. The label 'Côtes du Rhône' is seen more and more in restaurants, deservedly so. Rhône wine is sound, clean and full; it is strong and flavoury, and certainly far safer to buy than much ordinary Beaujolais. The great majority of the wines are red. The most subtle of them (though none are really delicate) are the *Côte Rôtie* wines in the north, not far below Lyons; they have a faint raspberry flavour and those which are a blend from the two slopes called the 'Côte Blonde' and the 'Côte Brune' are held to be best. There is also a very small production of an elegant white wine called Condrieu nearby. Further south, just before one reaches Valence, is the hill of *Hermitage*, terraced like a Babylonian garden, which produces admirable red and white wines, far to be preferred to a great deal of dearer burgundy. I have a pleasant recollection of being left to consume placidly a whole bottle of Hermitage to myself, my friends having rejected it as probably 'some South African wine' and dividing between the three of them a thin and falsely-labelled Beaune. Crozes-Hermitage, next to it, produces wines considered to be slightly inferior; I have not found this so.

All the Rhône wines have a distinguishing characteristic, which is most marked in the most popular of them, the *Chateauneuf du Pape*, produced much further south, between the old Roman city of Orange and the Papal fortress of Avignon. It is a full-bodied warmth, a torridity, as if the heat of the Southern sun which had ripened and strengthened the grapes had been preserved and carried through into the bottles. Sometimes, the Châteauneuf can be coarse; it always is a wine to drink with strong-tasting food. Delicate tasting meats it would smother, but all those excellent dishes, reeking of garlic and swimming in oil, which are called 'something *Provençale*' on the menus have no better companion. Eat them and drink Châteauneuf; you will be as grossly happy as Tartarin in Tarascon. Moreover, this amiable centre-forward of a wine has a great tolerance of rough treatment: it is almost the only wine which is totally uninjured by railway travel and can be drunk in a jerking restaurant car with perfect contentment. There are few châteaux here; note Domaine de Mont-Redon. There is a little white Châteauneuf of which only Ch. Rayas has interested me. Opposite it –

Châteauneuf is grown on the east bank of the Rhône – are the fields which produce the only French rosé wine which has an international reputation. *Tavel* is both dry and fruity at once, has something of a bouquet, and travels well. All rosés are a pretty colour; Tavel is perhaps the prettiest.

As one proceeds further south, it becomes uncomfortably clear that the region of great wines has been left behind. Eastwards, along the Riviera, are the Côtes de Provence which produce several wines sold in odd-shaped bottles with rapturously-phrased tickets hung round their necks, but of the small delimited areas only one, *Cassis*, deserves separate mention. The white and rosé wines of this little seaside town have an individual flavour that goes well with mussels, oysters and sea-urchins; but they do not travel well. Westwards the prospect is worse; the torrent of *vin du Midi* which comes mostly from the area called Languedoc is in quantity and quality such that recurrent political crises are caused by the refusal of the French working class to drink it up. Only the high authority of the late P. M. Shand causes me to recommend that you should give St Georges d'Orcques of Languedoc a trial. Further round the coast are Frontignan, with a muscatel wine, and a group of indifferent sweet wines made around Perpignan, called Rivesaltes, Roussillon, Grenache, and Banyuls. They are mentioned here in warning, for their only use would be to placate a travelling companion who was desperate for something like an English public-house 'wine of port character' after his meal.

There is much more character in the wines of *Arbois*, in the Jura, than in most of the minor 'appellations'. They have a rather apple-like taste, and the whites and rosés are more interesting than the reds; the most interesting of them all is the expensive Château Chalon which is made somewhat in the manner of sherry, and tastes not unlike it. As it is impossible to get a good glass of sherry in France, this is worth knowing when you are travelling; but at the price asked the wine is hardly worth importing.

Of the remaining 'appellations' three are worth noting. On the slopes of the Pyrenees Jurançon is made; it is white, highly aromatic and sweet (though some dry Jurançon is now being made). Henry IV of France preferred Jurançon and Arbois to any other wines in his kingdom. In the centre of the Albigensian country is the still, clean, white, inexpensive wine of Gaillac.

Circling round the Bordeaux area north and west, but just not good enough to be included, are the wines of Bergerac in the Dordogne; best known are Montravel and Montbazillac; the latter is called the 'poor man's Sauternes', which is a sufficient description of it.

5. Champagne and other Sparkling Wines

Still champagne – Method of manufacture – Effects – Types of champagne – Shippers – Other sparkling wines.

IN all still wines there is a gradation. The finest château-bottled Cru Classé of Médoc is connected by an insensible progression with the Bordeaux ordinaires which the French worker drinks with his meal. Nowhere is there a sharp break: the progress has been an almost insensible process of acquiring desirable qualities and refining away coarseness and harshness. There used to be no such gradation in sparkling wines. There was champagne; sharply different, and a long way below it, were all other sparkling wines. Then champagne was a perfectionist wine; a subtle and balanced blend. Nowadays the single vineyard 'grower champagne', made to compete in roadside sales with the nearby mousseux, is often an ill-balanced, indifferent wine. Meanwhile, more sophisticated vinification – often by the champagne method – has produced French mousseux of vastly improved quality, at lower prices. Though they can never match a quality champagne, they are more acceptable than the all too plentiful bad champagne.

Champagne is made in the old province of that name – the 'dusty plain' (champagne pouilleuse, *campania pulverulenta*; not 'lousy plain'). By nature, it is a still wine; the Sillery which Thackeray's characters drank by the bucket was a refreshing and invigorating red or white wine with a taste of its own. A fair amount of still cham-

97

pagne, legally now described as 'Coteaux Champenois', is drunk in France. It is a clean drink, never a great wine. Unlike the sparkling, it is often local: those from Vertus-le-Mesnil, Bouzy and (still the best) Sillery are among the most familiar. Sparkling champagne, on the other hand, is sold on the name of its maker. For it is blended: when a year is found upon the label, this means that mainly, but not solely, the wines of that year have been used to make up the blend. But the wines of many vineyards – not uncommonly twenty or more – will have been used to create the grande marque.

The classification sponsored by the National Committee on Appellations allows many vineyards, some high up the Aube, the title of 'champagne'. But the vineyards that are important for the making of good champagne are those along the valley of the Marne from Château Thierry to a little beyond Epernay, those running some twelve miles south of that town (the 'Côte des Blancs'), and those on the long low plateau called the Mountain of Rheims. The grapes are usually black, but their juice is pressed swiftly, the skins are not retained during fermentation, and none of their colour comes through with the wine. Some wine is made from white grapes only; it is called *blanc des blancs* and experts can taste the difference. 'Pink champagne' is made by pouring in some red. Champagne ferments in the usual way in cask, until it ceases to ferment during the winter. When a second fermentation is due to take place in the spring, an elaborate procedure is gone through, said to have been perfected in the seventeenth century by Dom Perignon, a Benedictine monk. The various wines are blended, according to the judgment of the *chef de cave*, into what is known as a *cuvée*. Into this blending, this calculation not only of what the wines are but what they will be in five or ten years' time, goes the art and experience of the firm. The wine is next bottled in strong bottles with corks especially firmly attached, and its second fermentation takes place inside the bottles. During the ensuing months the bottles are slowly tilted from their horizontal position until they are standing on their heads. This causes the sediment thrown by the wine to slide slowly down towards the cork. When this process is complete, the neck of the bottle is frozen, and a lump of ice, made up of wine and dirt, is withdrawn. Sometimes the neck is not frozen, and the cork and dirt extracted by hand. In either case, the bottle foams, and is swiftly put under a machine which 'doses' it with a small percentage of syrup made of sugar melted in old champagne, and recorks it. The amount of syrup depends on what type of champagne is wanted. 'Brut', the driest, will have none, or less than 1 per cent of syrup; 'Extra Dry', the next driest, 1 to 2 per cent; 'Sec' or 'Gout Americain', which we should not call dry at all, 3 to 6 per cent; 'Demi-sec', 7 to 10 per cent; 'Doux', which used to be a Russian favourite, up to as much as 15 per cent. The actual amount varies year by year, of course, according to the quality and sweetness of the untreated wine. Once this operation, which is called *dégorgement* or throat-clearing, is completed, champagne is made. The after-life of some marques is short, after the air has got to it; some should be drunk within a few years of *dégorgement* so a knowledge of champagne years is relatively unimportant; what matters is the date of *dégorgement* and that you are rarely told except in the case of Bollinger 'R.D.' – recently disgorged. However, since it is only 'degorged' when due for despatch, the date of landing will do, and that you sometimes can find out. Anyway, it's not worth while keeping any champagne but the best in your cellar. It won't improve and it may go off.

A way of telling if champagne is at its peak is to look at the cork after it is drawn. If it has only just been 'degorged', the cork will go back almost to its original form of a straight pillar. If it has been very long in bottle, the stem of the cork will stay hard and narrow, like a piece of wood. The ideal shape is when the cork-stem fans out at the bottom, and the cork looks like a toadstool which has splayed out at the foot. But the bottle has to be opened before you can use this test.

The wine is dear, partly because so much work goes into its preparation, partly because it has for a century been a symbol in Anglo-Saxon countries for ostentatious self-indulgence. Puritanism in decay no longer persecutes sinfulness, it makes money out of it; governments therefore have put a specially high tax on this wicked wine. Millgirls (says the Treasury in effect to Sir Jasper the Bad Baronet) must of course continue to be ruined by you, twirling your moustache and offering them bottles of 'bubbly'; but to mark our disapproval you shall pay us an extra tax per foaming bowl.

The shipper's name is the only guide to the quality of the wine; here, then, is a list of the chief established firms. The choice is so much a matter of opinion that the only fair thing is to give the names in alphabetical order:

Bollinger, Alfred Gratien, Charles Heidsieck, Irroy, Krug, Lanson, Mercier, Moët & Chandon, Mumm, Perrier-Jouet, Piper Heidsieck, Pol Roger, Pommery & Greno, Roederer, Ruinart, Salon, Taittinger, Veuve Clicquot. The 'T' is pronounced in Moët and in Jouet.

There are many lesser-known houses which make excellent champagne – Venoge, Montebello, Castellane and Decaux are among the names I recall with pleasure. In buying lesser-known brands a good rule of thumb is to prefer the dated, or *millesimé*, wines to the non-vintage. 'In good years all champagne is good'; but in worse years the smaller houses do not always have enough stocks for blending to keep their standard up.

A very interesting exception to the rule that champagnes are blended is Mailly, which is made by the co-operative society of the wine growers in that village exclusively from their own grapes. Mailly is admittedly among the very best of the champagne vineyards, and I have always found the vintage Mailly admirable, and level with all but the best of the famous cuvées.

The other French sparkling wines can be treated more summarily. Probably the most attractive is Dry Regal, the sparkling Saumur of which Ackerman-Laurence make a speciality, or that of Seyssel in Savoy which Varichon & Clerc provide. There are also innocent and inexpensive sparklers from the Rhône area (St Peray and Clairette de Die), Clairette de Gaillac from that district, and Blanquette de Limoux from Languedoc.

Sparkling hock and sparkling moselle, in Germany called *Sekt*, have rather more character than these, and brands which one can commend are made by Deinhard, Kupferberg and Söhnlein Rheingold. Italy makes the rather sweet sparkling Asti Spumante, and Yugoslavia wines with fancy titles like Duc de Slovénie; both Australia and the United States produce sparkling white wine of which the best is Australian, called mysteriously 'Great Western', as though it were a railway wine. Sparkling red burgundy, with raspberry foam, is also made; but none of these wines has the bouquet and few the flavour of average champagne.

6. Rhenish

Character of Rhine wines – Meaning of German phrases – Moselles – List of Moselles – Hocks – List of Rhine wines – Alsatians.

THE final and convincing reason for classifying Hocks, Moselles, Alsatians and Stein wines altogether and calling them Rhenish, as our forefathers did, is that all the wines of the great basin of the Rhine have common characteristics; they are, in fact, only modifications of the same type of wine. Firstly, nearly all the wine is white; there are hardly any reds. There are Monkeyvale (Affenthaler), and Ahr Valley from Baden, two red hocks from Assmanshausen and Walporzheim (maybe others) which are on the level of a moderate Beaujolais and a hundred years ago were considered good sleeping draughts; and that is about all one can say for them. Secondly, they all develop when they are good an astonishing flowery bouquet which is unparalleled throughout the world. Thirdly, their taste is similar. Their fault, when they have one, is thinness; but even in thin Rhenish there lingers a memory of that individual taste. Only an expert can tell a hock from a moselle, but any new boy can soon distinguish a Rhenish wine from any other white in the world. Not to be mincing about it, they are the finest white wines in the world.

They should be drunk young. The 'big' hocks will attain considerable age from time to time, but they are rare; it is a risk to keep any bottle more than seven years. Moselles particularly have a young freshness which is easily lost.

They are dear, for the production is always below the demand, and the vineyards, especially of Moselle, extend so far north that weather disasters often ruin the crop.

It would confuse an already confused issue to discuss German wine labels prior to 1971 when, after many years of debate, Germany introduced new wine laws to protect the consumer and simplify labels, which formerly bore any of a dozen now forbidden commendatory terms. These laws divided German wine generally into three classes – two of them subdivided; gave the wine, not the vineyard, approved status: and reduced the number of named sites from about 26,000 to 3,000. The first classification describes wine which does not meet quality requirements simply as 'Wein', not entitled to a local name. The class satisfying the basic quality control is Tafelwein (table wine), divided into simple Tafelwein which need not contain any German wine, but is made from any EEC wines, even though blended, so long as they come from the same zone; and Deutscher Tafelwein which is 100 per cent. German and may take the geographical name of an area which provides 75 per cent. of the grapes. Most exported German wine is the finer Qualitätswein (quality wine) or Qualitätswein mit Prädikat (quality wine with special attributes). These must be made of approved grapes grown in one of the eleven quality areas and exhibiting its qualities; reach the required alcohol content; and be approved by a tasting panel. All Qualitätsweine are given a control (approval) number which is printed on the label with the name of their region, sub-region, town and, so long as 75 per cent. of the grapes come from the smallest area, vineyard-group or single vineyard, the grower, bottler and – if 75 per cent. applicable – the grape and vintage.

The six 'predicates', in ascending order of sweetness and price, are:

>*Kabinett,* made from mature grapes of a delimited area without added sugar;
>
>*Spätlese,* from late-picked and, therefore, very sweet grapes;
>
>*Auslese,* from selected bunches of late-picked grapes;
>
>*Beerenauslese,* from individually selected berries with the 'noble rot' or, at least, over-ripe;
>
>*Trockenbeerenauslese,* except in unusual climatic conditions, only from grapes with noble rot; rare, desperately expensive, yet usually produced at a loss.

plus *Eiswein;* also rare; made from grapes gathered and pressed while frozen.

All these six terms should indicate a full and scented wine, the product of the *pourriture noble* which produces an even more astonishing result here than in Sauternes.

There is one word, and a very common one, which carries no true guarantee of origin or character. It is 'Liebfraumilch', once the name of the wine of the Liebfrauenkirche at Worms, but which now means nothing but that the wines used to make it comes from somewhere in the Rhineland apart from the Middle Rhine; and it must satisfy Qualitätswein standards. Most merchants, because it is so popular and heavily advertised, have to have their own Liebfraumilch; there is nothing wrong in selling it but experts do not love it. Moselles are customarily bottled in green bottles, hocks in red-brown. Memorizing this simple fact has gained many a modest man the reputation of being what the Germans call a *Feinschmecker,* able to tell a moselle from a hock by one sip.

The Rhenish wine area consists of the vineyards by or near the great River Rhine, a short way up its minor tributaries the Ahr, the Lahn, the Main, the Nahe and the Neckar, on its great tributary the Moselle, and on *its* minor tributaries the Ruwer and the Saar. Little is grown north of the junction of the two great rivers at Coblenz. In the south, the vast majority of wine is grown on the French side of the river, in Alsace.

The MOSELLE area begins, theoretically, in the French department of Meurthe and Moselle, but there are no moselles of importance in France. Like so many small wines they are charming in their home country, but do not travel; I have, however, tasted in England good wine from Toul. As the river passes into Luxembourg (of which it is the border) the wine improves and the distinctive taste and bouquet of moselle becomes more perceptible. Remich and Wormelding are names worth noting; but we do not reach the fine moselles until we come to the odd-named town of Wasserbillig ('cheap water'). From here down to Coblenz there is a sequence of famous names. The vineyards have slatey soil, and little of it; they hang on to the rocky sides of the banks that the river writhes between, they are repeatedly blighted by frosts and deprived of sun. Yet the light-greenish wines that they produce have an almost unique finesse and bouquet.

To guide anyone among these wines is almost as difficult as to guide him among the cheaper Bordeaux; despite the new classifications the abundance of Rhenish vineyards is still overwhelming. To give a list of towns alone (as I did in previous editions) is not adequate help for, particularly in the moselles, to know the vineyard name is usually imperative. Therefore, it seems best to list, going down river, each town or village which produces to my knowledge excellent moselle, followed by the names of vineyards whose wine I have myself tasted and approved. The list, that is, is a personal list and incomplete. I wonder respectfully at (without wishing to imitate) the confidence of those writers – I do not mean professionals like the late and admired Alfred Langenbach – who once printed lists covering all the many vineyards, and estimated every one. I begin with the tributaries, the rivers Saar and Ruwer, and go on down the Moselle itself: giving post-1971 names:

SAAR

Ockfen (Bockstein, Herrenberg, Kupp)
Ayl (Kupp, Herrenberg)
Wawern (Herrenberger, Goldberg)
Wiltingen (Scharzhofberger)
Kanzem (Schlossberg)
Oberemmel (Rosenberg, Hutte)
Konz (Falkensteiner, Hofberg)
Avelsbach (Kupp)

RUWER

Waldrach (Meisenberg, Hubertusberg, Doktorberg, Krone)
Kasel (Lorenzberg, Kernagel, Held)
Grünhaus (Maximin Grunhaüser)
Eitelsbach (Karthaüser Hofberg, Herrenberg, Marienholz)

MOSELLE

Longuich (Maximiner, Herrenberg, Hirschlay)
Thörnich (Enggass, Ritsch)
Trittenheim (Apotheke, Altaerchen)
Dhron (Hofberger)
Piesport (Goldtropfchen, Günterslay, Falkenberg, Michelsberg, Domherr)

Wintrich (Stefanslay)
Brauneberg (Juffer, Hasenläufer)
Lieser (Niederberg, Helden, Rosenlay)
Bernkastel (Doktor, Graben, Schlossberg, Rosenberg, Lay, Bratenhofchen)
Wehlen (Sonnenuhr, Nonnenberg, Klosterberg)
Graach (Abstberg, Himmelreich, Domprobst)
Zeltingen (Schlossberg, Himmelreich, Sonnenuhr)
Urzig (Schwarzlay, Wurzgarten)
Trabach (Hühnerberg)
Kröv (Nacktarsch)
Reil (Goldlay, Falklay, Heissenstein, Sorentberg)
Zell (Geisberg, Kreuzlay, Pommereu)

Bernkastel is the most famous name on the Moselle, and the lately enlarged Doktor the most famous vineyard. Divided between three owners – Deinhard, Lauerburg and Thänisch – it must be the most valuable slate and shale slope in the world. During the sixties a series of locks was being made all along the river Moselle to make it navigable, and conservatives were grumbling because of the noise and dust, and the ultimate disappearance of the quiet of the valley. The noise and dust were soon gone, the wider quite smooth stretches of water now add to the beauty of the valley, the sun reflected from them now gives us all better wine, more wine and more frequent good vintages, and the barges going up and down the river have brought life to the little towns again.

Turning to the south at Coblenz and going up the Rhine, we are in the region of the HOCKS, but no great wines are to be found until we reach Lorch on the east bank, at the beginning of the district called the *Rheingau*. This small area ranks as one of the four fabulous wine-growing regions of the world – the others are the slopes of the Côte d'Or, the grey fields of the Haut-Médoc, and the Hungarian hill of Tokay. Crowded together are a dozen famous names: Erbach, Geisenheim, Hallgarten, Hattenheim, Johannisberg, Oestrich, Rauenthal, Rudesheim, Kiedrich, Eltville, Steinberg and Winkel. Hochheim, some little way away on the Main, which may perhaps have given its name to hock, is of the same type. It was in this area that the method of making the finest hocks was first discovered. It is said to have been an accident; at the Schloss Johannisberg, the most famous single vineyard (the story goes) the drunken and absentee clerical owner failed to send the order for harvesting in 1775 until the grapes had rotted on the vine. The corrupt mass was despairingly pressed and the casks pushed aside; in a couple of years' time the peasants discovered in them a wine better than they had ever known.

The following are the wines which I personally have drunk and can commend in the dozen places just named.

RHEINGAU

Eltville (Sonnenberg, Rheinberg, Tauberberg)

Erbach (Marcobrunn, Honigberg, Siegelsberg, Steinmorgen)

Geisenheim (Rothenberg)

Hallgarten (Jungfer, Schönhell, Hendelberg)

Hattenheim (Steinberg, Nussbrunnen, Engelmannsberg, Wisselbrunner, Hassel, Heiligenberg)

Hochheim (Domdechaney, Kirchenstück, Hofmeister)

Johannisberg (Schloss Johannisberg, Mittelhölle, Vogelsang, Klaus)

Kiedrich (Gräfenberg, Sandgrube, Wasseros)

Oestrich (Doosberg, Lenchen, Magdalenengarten, Klostenberg)

Rauenthal (Baiken, Rothenberg, Nonnenberg, Gehrn)

Rüdesheim (Roseneck, Bischofsberg, Bergh Rottland, Klosterlay)

Winkel (Schloss Vollrads, Hasensprung, Dachsberg, Jesuitengarten, Klaus)

On the bank facing the Rheingau is the district of *Rheinhesse*, where the wines are slightly sweeter and softer, falling only a little short of the supreme virtues of the Rheingau. On the River Nahe are vineyards of a similar character. Here, with the same provisos and apology, is a list covering both areas.

NAHE

Bad Kreuznach (Narrenkappe, Bruckes)

Niederhausen (Rosenberg, Hermannshöhle)

Rüdesheim (Goldgrube, Weisberg)

Schloss Böckelheim (Kupfergrube, Felsenberg)

Waldböckelheim (Kronenfels)

RHEINHESSEN

Alsheim (Sonnenberg, Römerberg)

Bechtheim (Rosengarten)

Dienheim (Siliusbrunnen, Höhlchen)

Guntersblum (Steig, Autenthal)

Mettenheim (Schlossberg, Goldberg, Michelsberg)

Nackenheim (Rothenberg, Engelsberg, Gunderloch-Lange)

Nierstein (Pettenthal, Glock Holbe, Orbel, Olberg, Kirchplatte, Kranzberg, Findling, Hipping, 'Gutes Domtal' was a blend of any Niersteiners; now a section of vineyards, one in Nierstein and those of twelve other villages)

Oppenheim (Daubhaus, Sackträger, Kreuz, Paterhof)

Westhofen (Kirchspiel)

Worms (Liebfrauenstift)

Further south, there are the more luscious wines of the *Palatinate* or Pfalz; once again, here is a list, which is merely that of personal experience; there are undoubtedly excellent wines that I have not tried.

PALATINATE

Bockenheim (Goldgrube, Hassmansberg)

Deidesheim (Rennpfad, Hofstück, Kränzler, Vogelsang)

Dürkheim (Spielberg, Nonnengarten, Fronhof, Hochbenn)

Flemlingen (Zechpeter)

Forst (Jesuitengarten, Kirchenstück, Ungeheuer, Freundstuck)

Herxheim (Honigsach, Kirchenstück)

Kallstadt (Annaberg, Horn, Kirchenstück, Nill, Kronenberg, Steinacker)

Rhodt (Rosengarten, Schloss, Klosterpfad)

Ruppertsberg (Hoheburg, Spiess)

Wachenheim (Fuchsmantel, Gerümpel, Rehbächel, Altenberg).

Away from the Rhine to the east are the Franconian wines, called Stein wines and sold in elegant green flagons which before the last war held the full 75 centilitres that French wine bottles do, but since then have been silently contracted to the usual German 70 cl. They have a dry hard taste, very attractive indeed when one is used to it; but there are very few of them and they are quickly bought up. The bottles are called Boxbeutel, and the names to look for (if, outside Germany, you have the chance) are Randersacker, Iphofen, Thüngersheim and particularly Würzburger Leisten. There are also some good wines produced in Baden which began to be offered abroad in small quantities in the 1970s, especially that which comes from the district called the Emperor's Chair (Kaiserstuhl) or the village of Durbach.

Nothing else worthy of note is found as one goes up the Rhine except the ALSATIANS, which in the past have been regarded as essentially inferior to the German wines. This was unfair; there certainly was a period in which they were generally of lower quality, but they have immensely improved of recent years, and in 1962 were granted the classification of 'appellation controlée', which puts Alsace officially among the great wine regions of France. Moreover, though these wines are 'Rhenish' in character they have an individuality and differ more from hocks than, say, moselles or steinwein do; and it is absurd to expect from them the same taste. The flavour of an Alsatian is distinctive – it can be smelt most in a Muscat, tasted most in a Gewurztraminer. The bouquet is more forest-like, and the taste more earthy, than in a hock.

1959 was a vintage more remarkable here even than elsewhere in the Rhineland; it was this year that first put Alsatians among the great white wines.

The wines are still marketed almost always under the names of the grapes used, not the most helpful of classification, except maybe for wine merchants. The ordinary consumer will most probably recognise the taste of the unexpectedly dry Muscat, or Gewurztraminer (the prefix Gewurz means that the merchant or grower considers the wine 'spicy' in flavour) if not the others. For the record, these are the names of the vines: Chasselas (prolific, but not usually seen on labels) and Sylvaner which produce fairly ordinary wines; Muscat, Riesling, which Alsatians consider the finest, Tokay (not like Hungarian Tokay, and really a sort of Pinot) and Gewurztraminer which make 'nobler' wines. A mixture is called 'Zwicker', and a mixture of the finer grapes only is called 'Edelzwicker'. 'Gentil', a name not often seen now, also indicates a blend. It is not true that Alsatian wines will not last; I tasted in

1963 a sensational series of Alsatians ranging from 1900 to 1834 and they were all very much alive (the oldest was the liveliest). But there is no particular reason for hoarding them, especially as their freshness of taste is one of their chief merits. Gradually bottles with place names and vineyard names are appearing on the market – Ribeauvillé, Riquewihr, Barr, St Odile, Guebwiller, Eguisheim, Turckheim, Bergheim, Obernai, Ammerschwihr, are among the town names worth remembering; Clos des Amandiers and Clos des Sorcières among the vineyard names – but the names of shippers still are more important for the foreign buyer. Note therefore the names of Dopff et Irion, Dopff 'Au Moulin', Preiss-Henny, Zind-Humbrecht, Trimbach, Willm, Kuentz-Bas and Hugel; there are, of course, many other reliable *marques* and the standard of the co-operatives is uniformly good.

7. Still Wines of other Countries

Hungary: Tokay – Italy: Chianti – Switzerland – Spain – Portugal – Greece – Yugoslavia – Cape – Australia.

THERE is a lot of good wine in Chile, and in the United States there is a rapidly growing production of both red and white, some of it on the way to being excellent. The best is made in California; the considerable amount of wine produced east of the Rockies is of a different taste and sometimes made in part from wild local vines which give it what is politely called a 'foxy' taste (from, I suppose, the smell round a vixen's lair). But practically none has been exported since the Prohibitionists killed the flourishing Californian trade in 1919; and anyway, this is not a book about American wines. A separate study on that is needed; it is a growing and rapidly changing subject.

Of other countries HUNGARY shall come first. For it alone possesses a truly great wine, which is unique in the world. There are numerous fairly good white wines in Hungary particularly in the Balaton area, sometimes marketed under the name of the vine (Furmint), sometimes under local names such as St George, St Stephansberger, and Badacsonyi; a Riesling from Pecs which has appeared recently on Western markets is of very good character. A heavy dark red wine made particularly well at Eger, owes its fame largely to its name – Bikaver or 'Bull's Blood'. But it is none of these which has made Hungarian wine famous; it is *Tokay*. Fifty years of confusion and warfare have interfered with the making of this magnificent wine, have injured its quality often enough, and have sometimes cut it off from its foreign markets altogether. Its reputation for the West is thus partly made up of memory and legend. 'Imperial Tokay' no longer exists – it was wine from the 'K. und K.' vineyards near Tarczal – but musical comedy uniforms, memories of the Hapsburg court, and the tunes of Jerome Kern are still evoked by the name. Tokay – often pronounced to rhyme with O.K., and not, as it should be, with pop-eye – carries a suggestion of careless, harmless, gaudy, unreal gaiety; but it also offers more important encouragements. The doctors of the days of George IV, who should have known, and their successors well into the present century, considered it a proved restorer of virility, and at the same time an increaser of fertility. This view they enforced by remarkable examples from their own casebooks, unsuitable for quotation. However, it appears to be an admitted fact that Augustus the Strong of Saxony, who had 365 bastards, one for each day of the year, drank so much of it that he died. Usually, however, Tokay was credited with saving, not destroying, life. The late C. W. Berry, a very well-known London vintner who lived to an opinionated old age, had a large number of detailed anecdotes in which invalids near to death, and indeed actually *in extremis*, had been rallied and restored to life by two teaspoonfuls of Tokay *Essenz*. The great Dr Druitt recommended Tokay *Essenz* in cream to wives who had failed to provide their husbands with an heir.

Tokay is a golden wine grown in strictly delimited vineyards round the town of that name in the district of Hegyalja. It has a very distinctive taste of its own, and a peculiarly splendid bouquet which is fresh and in some way *green*, like young flowers and grasses in a spring meadow. There is an ordinary, dry table Tokay, called Pecsenyibor, which has a distinct recollection of the Tokay flavour in it, but it is rarely exported, and is often rather sharp when it is. The famous wine is that classified as Szamorodni, Aszu or Ausbruch, and Essenz. These classes are distinguished by the amount of over-ripe grapes which have been used to make the wine in each. The Furmint vine ripens very irregularly and both ordinarily ripe and almost raisin-like grapes will be found in the same field. A Szamorodni wine is made by pressing all the grapes together, as they come. An Aszu wine is made by a deliberate mixing of the two kinds; Aszu wines are classified by the number of the 'Puttonos' they contain, Puttonos being the containers in which the over-ripe grapes are collected. An Aszu of three Puttonos has only half as many as one of six Puttonos; it does not necessarily follow that it is only half as sweet, though it will have less of the distinctive Tokay flavour. The Essenz wine, very rarely seen now, is made exclusively from the juice which runs out from the over-ripe grapes under no greater pressure than their own weight. Even before the First World War as much as £2 would be paid for a single half-litre flask of this. Sweet, very aromatic, and quite low in alcoholic content, it was supposed to have curative powers approaching the magical. The earlier vintages now make high prices at auction.

ITALY makes more wine, and drinks more per head, than any other country in the world. There is much good wine though none of the quality of a distinguished claret or Burgundy. Public confidence in Italian wines was badly shaken by the scandalous quality of what was sent to Germany in the early sixties. As a result, the D.O.C. – Denominazione di Origine Controllata – wine laws, similar to Appellation Contrôlée in France, were passed in 1963. These and the introduction of the most modern equipment for large scale wine-making by wealthy firms or cooperatives, has improved the consistency and lifted the general standard of Italian wine-making, in the last few years, from a peasant craft to a sophisticated industry.

The best Italian wines come from the north. The most famous is Chianti, now always red, never white, generally recognized by its straw-covered flasks. That wine, though was often 'stretched' or blended with inferior grapes from other regions; at best it was an undistinguished, quick maturing, light wine. The best Chianti is found in Bordeaux-type bottles; it is the Chianti Classico, from that strictly limited district; skilfully made, long matured and identified by its seal of a black cockerel. Near to Chianti, and probably even finer, are the Brunello di Montalcino and the Vino Nobile di Montepulciano, both full bodied red Tuscan wines matured for four or three years in cask before bottling.

The red Santa Maddalena from the South Tyrol – where most of the wine is white – ages well in bottle and is much exported to Austria.

Piedmont produces not only the sparkling Asti Spumante but two of Italy's best red wines in Barolo and Barbaresco; the distinctive Gattinara and Ghemme; and sound reds in the Barbera, Freisa and Nebbiolo (all three called after their grape types).

The Verona district makes the most acceptable wines of Veneto; the dry white Soave; the dry red Valpolicella, Bardolino and Valpantena. The historic Valtelline reds from the foothills of the Alps, made almost entirely from the Nebbiolo grape, are light, scented and stylish; they go by such names as Valgella, Grumello, Inferno, Sforzato di Spina and Villa Perla. Orvieto, the classic sweet white wine of Umbria, is now often made dry in deference to modern taste. The Riesling Italico, Tocai, Malvasia and Pinot Bianco are palatable, well balanced dry white wines with over 12 per cent. of alcohol, from the Gorizia Hills.

Near to Rome are the white wines of Albano, and Castelli Romani, which have been steadily improving in the last twenty years, and the town of Montefiascone produces a white wine called Est! Est!! Est!!! It owes this name to a story, told in varying detail, of the journey of a German Bishop called to Rome for the election of a pope, who sent in advance of him his major-domo, to taste and find where there was good wine for his master. Where he found it, he was to mark *Est* ('there is') on the shutters. His Grace and his cortège arrived at Montefiascone, and along the main street found each shutter marked *Est*. 'Est'; 'Est'; 'Est'; up the street until in the square they found the major-domo stone dead from excessive attention to duty. Over his body they erected a tomb with the inscription:

> *Propter nimium Est Est Est*
> *Dominus noster mortuus est.*

(Through too much Est Est Est our chief is dead.)

Would that the wine was as pleasant as the story; but in truth it is undistinguished.

As we go further south, in the hotter sun the wines get stronger and fruitier; they also get more volcanic. The wines of Capri (from Capri, Ischia and the mainland nearby) and the Neapolitan Vesuvio and Lacrima Cristi ('Christ's tear') show these characteristics markedly. Though there are no great wines here, bad wines are rare. Falerno, Horace's Falernian, once the best wine in all the world, is a mortifying disappointment; it is not bad, it is just characterless, living on testimonials two thousand years out of date.

In Sicily good strong plain wine comes from Etna and

Syracuse, and the Corvo red and white from near Palermo is beginning to show great individuality; the most important wine of Sicily, however, is Marsala, which is dealt with in the next chapter.

The technological advances in wine-making which have had such important effects in the south and Sicily may soon be reflected in Italy's expanding export market.

In SWITZERLAND there is a small production of mostly good wine, the wines in the Eastern cantons being in general of lower quality than the Western. The commonest name, Fendant, is that of a vine – also called Chasselas. Wine from the 'Johannisberg' (that is Sylvaner) grape is usually better, and the whites are all better than the reds. The rosé is good also, but by Swiss law must not be called rosé but Partridge Eye (Oeil de Perdeix). The wines have a slightly apple-like taste like the Arbois wines. The best come from the Valais (round Sion), the Vaud (the districts of Chablais, La Côte, and Lavaux) and Neuchatel; the Genevan wines are rapidly improving, especially those from the area called Mandement. The wines of Yvorne and Delazey I have found particularly good, and a 1958 Aigle had a bouquet like a moselle while it was still in cask. Swiss wines, like the nation, are reliable; but they too are not low-priced, never brilliant, and there aren't many of them. They do, however, have one distinction. A number of the white wines, notably the Fendant du Sion, become naturally *pétillant*, half-sparkling and when they do this they develop a flavour which is particularly their own, and particularly pleasing.

The greatest wine of SPAIN is sherry, already described; the dessert wines of Malaga and Tarragona are mentioned later. The consistently reliable and available table wine is Rioja, made under strict control of quality and district, in Castile. Most, and the best, of it is red; and whether light (in claret type bottles) or heavier (burgundy bottles) it is good quality-for-money value at all levels. Even the finest, like the Marqués de Riscal or any of half a dozen other bodegas, is not dear. Other good Spanish bottles are Panadés (red) and Alella (sweetish white) from Catalonia. The full, strong, red Alicante used to be a world-wide favourite; it will make you drunker than you think. Some sparkling wines are skilfully made by the champagne method at Codorniu.

The Spanish wines most often seen in Britain, though, come from the bulk areas of La Mancha, Valdepeñas and Tarragona. These are the wines which, often blended or sweetened, were long exported by Spanish merchants in pursuit of a quick peseta, labelled Spanish Chablis, Spanish Burgundy, Spanish Sauternes, or even Spanish Champagne. When that was stopped by law, they adopted brand names. Sometimes they are good ordinaires, sometimes not. They pretended for so long to be what they were not that it is impossible now to say what they are, or what they might be.

The most satisfactory contrast to them is to be found across the frontier, in PORTUGAL. In the last dozen years an enormous amount of thoroughly sound table wines, white, red and pink, have been exported from Portugal; and Portuguese laws compel them to be offered under their true names. Our grandfathers knew Colares, Bucelas and others and kept them in their cellars; so there was a tradition to call on. Bucelas is a light dry white wine, Colares a strong harsh red wine needing keeping, reaped from vines whose roots may strike 14 feet down through sand. Dão, pronounced Downg, is a mountainous area producing full and strong red and white wines which are strictly controlled, of a distinctive character and may have a great future as cultivation is improved. The best known brand exported is Grão Vasco. The upper Douro area, where port comes from, also produces good red and white table wines; brands worth noting at Evel and Vila Real (from the town of that name). Other less distinguished districts are Alcobaça and Ribatejo. 'Grandjó' (a slurring of the name Grandja of Alijo) and Moscatel de Setubal are sweet dessert white wines; Edward VII is said to have liked them. Periquita, a coarse red ordinaire, is named from its grape, so also are the two Bastard wines ('White Bastard' and 'Brown Bastard', authentic Elizabethan names) put on the English market in the sixties by the firm of Rosenheim, which however permitted its more timorous customers to ask for 'Santos Bar Sinister'. The most interesting of all Portuguese table wines, however, come from the Minho district in the extreme north-west and are called Green Wines (*vinhos verdes*). They are drunk very young, while they still have a sort of 'prickle' which makes them rather less than half-sparkling. They are numbered and have a state label of authenticity, and they should be poured briskly into the glass, to excite the pétillance; then they are exhilarating. I have tasted the red *vinho verde*, but it is an acquired taste; the best are white; note Alvarinho de Monçao, Casal Garcia, and Lagosta. Portuguese pinks are quite good, and are becoming popular, but they are less interesting, with the exception of those which are half-sparkling, like a green wine.

In GREECE what were in classical times excellent wines and could be again are regularly ruined by being made into 'retzina' – that is, flavoured with rosin or pinegum. The taste for this can be acquired, but there is no need to acquire it. The wines that escape this process are rarely distinguished. A good deal of red Samian wine used to be exported before the Second World War, particularly to Germany, which is short of red wines; but those who tasted it were inclined to take Byron's advice and 'dash down yon bowl of Samian wine.' The Rhodian wines are better than most; the 'Chevalier de Rhodes' is the best wine to order when you are on holiday. Mavrodaphne, for all its charming name, is a heavy and undistinguished wine 'of port character'. CYPRUS wines are what Greek wines would be less ill-treated. There is an adequate dessert wine called Commandaria, some passable sherry and a strong dry white wine called Aphrodite.

The table wines which have risen fastest and most deservedly in popularity since the first edition of this book are those of YUGOSLAVIA. The most famous area is in the republic of Slovenia, whose capital is Liubliana, and its name is Lutomer. (I am spelling these names as nearly as possible as they are spoken; the eccentricities of the *srpsko-hrvatsei* alphabet are nationalistic obstacles which only discourage would-be drinkers). The Lutomer wines are generally marketed under their grape-names, as in Alsace: Sylvaner, Sauvignon, Riesling (the most popular), Traminer (the best, as I think), Shipon (an odd native vine). Rumenski Muskat (called Golden Muscat) has a high muscatel scent.

One of the few estates whose wines are sold separately is Jeruzalem, which owes its name to the ingenuity of some artful Crusaders who reconciled their oath to 'go to Jerusalem' with their intention to stay indefinitely sozzling themselves here; they merely compelled the local serfs to re-name their village 'Jeruzalem'. At the northernmost point of the wine-field is the small town of Radgona, where from the Ranina grape they made a sweet wine to which the label 'Tigermilk' has been attached. Sold young, it is very syrupy, but I have drunk in Radgona itself a 1947 Ranina wine which had gone orange and developed a fine series of flowery flavours.

The next most interesting white wine is called Zhilavka, and comes from Herzegovina and Macedonia; it has a granitey, mountainous taste and in my experience is better several hours after opening. Of red wines the easiest on foreign palates come from a district whose name unfortunately is Brda but the bottles carry also the names of the grapes, Merlot or Cabernet; the wine is like a superior Chianti. Further inland is a heavy Serbian wine called Prokupatz, not really notable, and the locally popular Istrian wine called Teran, dark purple and harsh, is only suited to Balkan bandits. The Dalmatian red wine, which has a general name of Plavatz, is much pleasanter. The best comes from the peninsula of Pelyesatz and has, not unreasonably, been given fancy names like Castle Dalmain and Pelesco, and the best within that area is said to come from the small town of Dingatch.

Three other countries' wines deserve notice. *Bulgarian* wines first began to be sold freely in the West in 1969, and their quality was surprising. Like the Yugoslavs they are named after vines: the best white is the delicate Chardonnay and the best red the Cabernet. The most individual is the very dry Misket; the Bulgar favourite, the Gamza, is dull. *Russian* wines began to appear in small quantities on the market in the sixties; they were Georgian in origin, honest and cheap but less distinguished. Mukazani was the best red and Tsinandali the white. *Austrian* wines had more character, but were still to be classed as small wines. Kalterersee from the Tyrol was a good red, very acceptable in Germany where there is a dearth of reds; the best whites come from the Wachau area. Schluck is usually a good plain wine; Gumpoldskirchner rather better; Schloss Grafenegg better still.

More important than any of these last are the vineyards of South Africa and Australia, the only areas (except California) from which there is an early hope of new sources of good wine to supply the steadily increasing population of the world. South Africa, more correctly, euphoniously and traditionally called the CAPE, has a longer history. Its history as a wine-producer starts in the last years of the seventeenth century. Its wines improved in quality and quantity in the eighteenth century, and in the 1820's 'Cape Red' and 'Cape White' were regularly quoted in London wine merchants' lists. Mr Godfree, of Arthur Godfree Ltd., once showed me an 1828 list in which they were priced only a trifle below comparable French wines. But in the nineteenth century the principles of 'free competition' so dragged down not only the price but the quality of Cape wines that they acquired an evil name on the London market. Only during the First World War (in the year 1917, to be exact) was an effort made to safeguard quality and, of course, price. From that year dates the dominance of the K.W.V. which includes a trifle under 85 per cent. of the winegrowers of the Cape. (The initials are those of the Afrikaner words meaning 'Co-operative Winegrowers' Association'.) From it, Cape wines have derived the advantages and disadvantages of mass production. The bad wines, which did the trade so much harm, have been expelled from the export trade. Prices, as the 'handouts' of the Association rather tactlessly emphasize, have been kept up. High standards of wine-making – though not of wine-drinking – have been enforced; the latest scientific methods of wine-making are employed. But, as always happens when wines are made, or blended, in great quantities, there are few distinguished wines. Cape red and white table wines are strong, clean and odourless. The red are less pleasing: the Steen and Rhine Riesling grapes produce some fresh white wines. Individual wines worth noting are: Bellingham Rosé, Zonnebloem Cabernet (red), Stellenrood (red), Drostdy (white), La Residence Alto (red), Vlakkenberg (red), and Nederburg (white). Paarl and Drakenstein are district names, of plain white wines. *Pontac* wine is sweet and heavy. Much more wine and some say, better dessert wine come from the huge wineries of *Stellenbosch*, where incompetent British generals were sent in the Boer War. ('Stellenbosched' is the English translation of 'Limogé'.) The most famous name in South African wines, however, is *Constantia*. Simon van der Stel planted these vineyards near Wynberg, at the end of the seventeenth century; they are as good as they are old. In his day the vineyards were divided only into Groot (Great) and Klein (Little) Constantia; since then the name Oude (Old) Constantia has appeared on bottles. That, though, is a dessert wine, hardly encouraged by the control legislation of 1974 which imposed a 2 per cent. sugar-limit.

AUSTRALIA is at once the hope and the despair of the wine-drinker. The condition for the production of good wine is the existence of a wine-drinking public in the country itself. The reason for the pre-eminence of French and German wines is not merely the law, but the existence of a large, informed, and critical wine-drinking public. The average Frenchman or German will not allow the wine producers to sell bad wine; if they do, he sees they get into trouble. The Italian does not mind if his wine is coarse, the Spaniard and the Portuguese is too poor to have a choice, the Greek likes his wine to taste of turpentine – those facts, and not any fault of nature, are to blame for the lower qualities of their wines. Now until the Second World War it could be said, with rough truth, that the Australian public was equally indifferent. It neither cared nor knew if the wine was good; it preferred whisky, anyway. But in the last quarter century the Australians have realized where their treasure is: they now drink four times as much wine as they did. In principle, this is excellent; it provides, that is, hope for a great wine industry. However, since the vintners can sell all their best wines at home, they mostly do not trouble to export them. They rely upon their standard lines of pre-war days. Some of these have a marked hard taste, due to the large amount of iron in them. As this may have some medical value in cases of anemia, it used to assure the Australians of support from the doctors.

But we do not all suffer from anemia, and in normal health our bodies will only absorb a limited amount of iron. Therefore, the sale of the 'ferruginous flagons' of Emu, Tintara, Big Tree, Keystone and so on have declined – relatively at least. Indeed, the importers would almost seem to have deliberately discouraged discriminating consumers. The 'flagon' itself, a screw-top container containing a bottle and a half, cannot be laid down to mature; no ordinary man can finish it at a sitting; the screw-top invites him to believe that it cannot be damaged by being opened, closed, and reopened for a week or more. As it may have been sent through the Red Sea in a hermetically-sealed metal tank it may well be so deadened that the inference is justified.

But there do exist very good Australian wines, and in the sixties an 'Australian Wine Centre' was opened in London to show them. A survey of them shows that two dangers lie in wait, and may yet prevent them occupying the rank they deserve among fine wines. One, which only Australians can deal with, is the capturing of vineyards which have achieved distinction by great firms which own prairies of vines and seem not even to know of the importance of local delimitations. Kirkton and Porphyry are only two names of what once were fine vineyards and are now mere 'brand names'. The second, oddly enough, is a lack of acid. A too-smooth wine matures, and dies, early; it cannot ever achieve the grandeur of an old burgundy or claret. Many (not all) Australian wines have this defect. One very attractive claret, a Stonyfell of 1951, which I was impressed enough by to bottle in my own home, developed an elephantine taste and bouquet like a Châteauneuf du Pape, but in five years collapsed into coloured water.

However, there are Australian wines which can achieve great age. I have drunk a startling 20-year-old 'St Cora' red, and an equally good Coonawarra 1938; a Penfold's Grange Hermitage of 1954 was even better, but (characteristically) the firm hardly ever offered this wine abroad. But there are firms whose wines are more easily found and well worth buying. Lindeman's even name their casks and number their bottles; their 'Gordowein' (made from Gordo grapes) is a white which has perfume and flavour; their Coolalta red (from the Coolalta vineyard) is like a good Rhône wine, but short-lived. The Cabernet grape crossed with the Shiraz produces a very good light claret; the Mildara (Victoria) and Seaview (South Australia) bottles, so labelled, are good. The latter firm, which has its vineyards in McLaren Vale, also offers a Riesling which reminds one of a *natur-rein* Rhenish wine. Hamilton's of Glenelg in South Australia produce a good 'Springton' Riesling, and a remarkable wine from the Ewell vineyards which they have damned in foreign eyes by calling it 'Moselle'. It is so light as to be almost colourless and it has a beautiful evanescent perfume – it is possibly the best Australian white wine I have ever drunk. Seaview, already mentioned, is another label which has acquired and deserves confidence. Tahbilk Estate has a name that has extended beyond Australia;

its Cabernet is an excellent claret, its Marsanne could be widely approved as a dry white wine to drink with fish or shellfish, and its Shiraz is a palatable red from pre-phylloxera vines.

8. Dessert Wines

Port – Madeira – Malaga – Marsala.

PERHAPS Tokay should have been included in this chapter, for most people treat it as a dessert wine. But in fact it would be possible to drink Tokay before and through as well as after a meal, nor is it a fortified wine. For that reason it has been described in Chapter VII. With Tokay removed, there can be no question which is the premier after-dinner wine: it is port. Brown sherry is sometimes taken instead; madeira, marsala and even malaga have their devotees; but on one thing the British working-class, middle-class and upper-class are agreed – that there's nothing like a good class of port. They have turned the upper reaches of the Douro almost into a British colony. All the vineyards of the 'Quintas' along its banks are devoted to growing the vines which will produce the grapes that will make the must which the population of Oporto, directly or indirectly, is engaged in blending into a drink which the British suburbs will approve, and which the Portuguese will either leave alone or sip with mild surprise. A complicated and, to a Latin, perverse procedure has to be gone through to produce this in some ways lovely and in some ways preposterous drink. The large firms use mechanical presses; but in the villages the rich, dark grapes (some white are used for white port) are often trodden in the old way. When the mantle (manta) of skins and solids forms on the top of the purple liquid, boys and men with linked arms prance up and down, breaking it up. (A Victorian author assured his readers that the songs sung at this wine-treading were censored by the Catholic priests and no indelicate verses were allowed.) Even after they have finished, 'monkey sticks' have to be used to break the blanket up. When fermentation has gone a certain way, the wine-maker adds a strong dose of brandy, which brings fermentation to an abrupt stop and holds a large amount of sugar in suspense. As much as one-fifth brandy is added, and another 5 per cent. may be added later. The wine, so treated, is almost undrinkable; and needs an unusually long time to mature, and to recover from its indigestion. This long time, and even more the skill of the Oporto shippers in blending, produces Port. Every Oporto merchant of importance holds great stocks of wine of varying ages which he uses to make his own blend. In his knowledge of how to mix them, and his skill in acquiring and maturing them, lies his claim to be a first-class shipper. Therefore, port is known, not by the name of its vineyard but by the name of its shipper.

By all the rules of language 'port' should be as English a word as 'claret'; but in Great Britain it is not so, for by the 1916 treaty with Portugal the word may only be applied to approved wine coming from the Upper Douro and exported over the bar at Oporto. The clumsy phrase 'port type' is therefore used for wines from other countries.

This much-loved, much-protected wine is divided into three classes. *Vintage* port is, as its name implies, made exclusively of grapes of a certain year. The shipper decides if a year is good enough for him to treat it as a vintage year and it would be a disaster for him to make a wrong choice. All the years, therefore, given in Chapter II are good years, and if a reputable shipper has shipped a year not mentioned there, it is safe to assume that for his wine at least that is a good year. A vintage port is bottled early, and left to mature for very many years. It was once a custom for a father on the birth of his eldest son to purchase some dozens of new port, which would be ready for the boy to drink when he was twenty-one.

Vintage port is dark, and throws a heavy 'crust'. All red wines form this film inside a bottle, which consists of various impurities of which the wine has rid itself during the years. But the crust of vintage port is of especial importance; the port is not fit to drink until the process which leads to forming the crust is complete, and the crust must not be broken up and shaken back into the wine. The bottles must lie undisturbed in the cellar, with the side on which there is a white splash uppermost. If decanted, the wine must be decanted most carefully, and no spot of muddy fluid allowed to pass. If it is left in the bottle, it must be handled gently and never jerked.

But all this trouble, and a not inconsiderable expense, leads to what in port-drinkers' opinion is the finest drink in the world. Even to others, it is incontestable that there is nothing like the series of tastes to be found in a fine vintage port. Moreover, appreciation of port is easily acquired. A taste for dry wines, even for the best claret, has to be learned; but even a newcomer will recognize the charm of the first taste of vintage port, and later, without trouble, he will learn to detect its after-taste and the more refined delicacies of its flavour. There is an endless and amicable dispute on whether port is best accompanied by cheese or by nuts; all devotees agree, however, that smoke ruins its flavour.

Port is sometimes described as 'old crusted' or 'vintage character'; this is port blended of several years, but treated as vintage port.

Tawny port is port of various years, blended and matured in cask. Wine in wood develops faster than in glass, for air cannot percolate through a bottle. Changes are faster, and more marked. Tawny port, therefore, soon loses the rich purple colour of vintage port, and is ready to drink much sooner. But though it never has the rich tastes of a vintage wine, it has all the essential port characteristics, and indeed is a pleasanter drink for people whom vintage port makes 'liverish'. Contrary to general belief, it does not improve much in bottle and there is no point in keeping it long in one's cellars.

Ruby port, on the other hand, does. It is a blend of early-bottled wines, usually rather sweeter than tawny. By the nature of things, there must be in it a rather high proportion of the wines not good enough to be used either for vintage or 'vintage character' wines. Most public-house port is of this type.

Recently, there have been two innovations in this tradition-bound trade. One is 'late bottled' vintage port, which is held six years or more in cask; it becomes lighter than the usual vintage port but tastes similar (not like tawny). The other is a dry – really dry – white port served cold as an apéritif.

The names of the most famous shippers – given in alphabetical order – are: Cockburn, Croft, Delaforce, Dow, Ferreira, Fonseca, Graham, Martinez, Offley, Rebello Valente, Smith Woodhouse, Taylor Fladgate, Tuke Holdsworth, Warre.

Of the Commonwealth wines which but for English law would undoubtedly be called 'port', recommendation has already been made of the South African Constantia. Some good wine is also made in Australia; in choosing it look for those brands whose makers refuse to submit to the insult of calling their wine 'port type' or 'port character'. Also, select tawny wines by preference, for it is easier to reproduce satisfactorily the process of making tawnies than vintage ports. I have found enjoyable: Stony-fell Dry Tawny, Seppellt's Para and Emu Vintage Tawny, though the word 'vintage' in the last name is unjustifiable.

OTHERS

AFTER port, the most famous fortified dessert wine is *Madeira*. Since Shakespeare's day, and even earlier, it has been a favourite English drink. But in those days it was an unfortified table wine. The earliest mention of fortification seems to be in 1753, when Francis Newton, a precursor of the present firm of Cossart Gordon, mentions that some of his unscrupulous rivals had poured 'a Bucket of brandy' into their pipes of wine to preserve them on their sea voyages. He was shocked at their wickedness; very soon he was doing the same thing himself. Madeira is naturally a rather light wine, with usually about 11 per cent. of alcohol, but nowadays nothing under 18 per cent. is exported.

Apart from this change the wine is commonly still made in a very strange manner, which can have changed very little since Zarco discovered the island in 1420. The grapes are pressed by men dancing on them in a sort of stone trough, sometimes to music, sometimes singing improvised songs. The residue is tied round with rope into a sort of pyramid, and pressed again, often by a tree trunk attached to a huge stone. Then, in an equally primitive process, the grape juice is poured into goatskins (with the hair inside) which men carry down the hillside to the vats, draping them round their necks. Now it is fermented into wine in the usual way, but, either before or after fortification, the casks are put into a sort of gigantic oven, called the *Estufa*; here the wine stays at a temperature and for a time determined by the shipper (subject to some legal limitations). It is also repeatedly stirred and shaken. The object of this strange procedure is to reproduce as closely as possible the conditions of a voyage to the East or West Indies in a small sixteenth-century ship. The result is a wine with a curious bittersweet taste, unlike any other, varying in colour from yellow to dark brown. It is most generally classified according to the grapes from which it is made. These 'special growths', in ascending order of sweetness, are Sercial (a very small bearer making an unusually pleasant wine, dry as madeiras go), Verdelho, Boal (pronounced Bual) and Malmsey, which is an Anglicisation of the native name Malvasia, which is in its turn a Venetian form of the Greek name of the vine in its original home. There is one place-name used, Camara de Lobos, a village where very good wine is made, mostly from the Tinta vine, and there may soon be another, Campanario, as that arid area was being irrigated in the early fifties.

But not all the labels on bottles found in Britain have either place-names or vine-names on them. Sometimes they only say vaguely 'Full Rich' or 'Fine Pale'. The purchaser has to rely upon the skill and honesty of the shipper; the best known names here are Avery, Cossart Gordon, Blandy, Leacock, Tarquinio Lomedino, Henriques, Rutherford & Miles. Wines I have personally liked are Avery's and Tarquinio's Soleras, Henriques' Ribeiro, and Leacock's Penny Black Malmesy.

Madeira is a wine of endless age. It can last a hundred and sixty years for sure – I have myself drunk some excellent authenticated wine of 1715 – and how much longer it can live nobody knows. Unfortunately, the earlier habit of bottling vintages has been abandoned, apparently about the time the phylloxera devasted the island in the 1870's. There still exist, few and high priced, some bottles of ancient vintages. If they come your way, you must drink them in a particular manner; gulp them, and you will find them bitter and indeed nasty. For time has turned them into a sort of essence. Take a small mouthful, hold it in your mouth and roll it round for the amount of time you need to breathe in and out twice through the nose, then let it trickle down your throat. You will find your whole mouth is perfumed with its extraordinary taste. This is a remarkable experience, and you should take a full ten minutes over the smallest glass of these venerable wines. There are dated Soleras, blended in the Spanish way, but the percentage of the original wine in any given Solera may be very small. During the Victorian age madeira was one of the most popular wines, in England and in New England, but it was eclipsed later. It has been coming back into favour since the fifties, and can be very agreeable at eleven o'clock with a slice of madeira cake, or at the beginning of a meal with a slice of melon.

Malaga, a Victorian favourite, is a fortified, very sweet Spanish wine made round the town of that name. It has a very heavy taste, and is dark in colour – sometimes almost black. *Marsala*, made in Western Sicily, is a fairly cheap, strong, brown dessert wine. It has a distinct sulphurous taste, possibly from the volcanic soil. It has always been blended to suit the English taste, ever since Nelson's officers and men acquired a taste for it in 1799. Woodhouse's London Particular is perhaps the best-known; there are other brands under the names of Ingham and Florio, but the differences are not great. The brand called 'Garibaldi' – after Garibaldi's landing at Marsala with his Red Shirts – is somewhat lighter.

There is a kind of imitation port made in Spain at *Tarragona* and another at *Lisbon*.

9. Spirits

Various: arrack, aquavit, vodka, slivovitz, calvados, marc – Gin – Rum – Brandy – Whisky – Liqueurs.

THIS is not an exhaustive study of spirits. If it were, it would have to cover the tipples of every nation in the world, including the strange drink which South Sea Islanders make by chewing cassava roots and spitting out the juice. Not all alien drinks are horrible; some are drinkable in civilized circumstances. There is a spirit popular all over the Near and Middle East, often called 'raki' or some other Levantine distortion. It has a real English name, which is *arrack*, and it used to be a favourite drink with eighteenth-century rakes. It ought to be made from rice or palm juice, tastes queer but not particularly disagreeable, is not good for you unless you suffer from a special form of vitamin-starvation, and was thought to be aphrodisiac. Lord Richard Grosvenor, the second worst 'blade' in the London of the 1770's, always used to order a bowl of hot arrack when about to complete a conquest. The Scandinavian *aquavit* or *snaps* can be made from almost anything, including notably ordinary potatoes. It is a colourless or pale yellow spirit with a slight taste of caraway. Of the Swedish and Norwegian aquavits, Norrlands, U.P. Andersson and Löitens are the best. The Danish I find smoother and with more taste; two are Aalborger (from the town where it is made) and the older Jubileeum. It should be drunk very cold and before, or with, lager. It is the only thing that I know which really does enhance the taste of beer. It prepares the palate to detect its quality; a beer which before then had seemed ordinary and dull suddenly acquires all the cerevisial virtues. *Vodka* also may be made of almost anything containing carbohydrate – potato, rye, or what you please. It is oily, very strong, deceptive, should be taken very cold and gulped. Don't take much of it without the small greasy *hors d'oeuvres* that the Russians call zakuski. The authentic Russian (Stolichnaya) and Polish (Wyborowa) vodkas have a different flavour from the British imitations such as Smirnoff or Cossack, which tend to taste of nothing. *Slivovitz* is a similar spirit made in the Balkans from plums, of which it has a faint reminder in its taste. *Klekovatz* is a slivovitz made with juniper. *Applejack* is distilled from cider; in France it is called *calvados* and comes from that department in Normandy – the best from the Vallée d'Auge. In most wine districts of France they distil a spirit from the mush left after the grapes have been pressed, called *marc*; addicts can find in the 'marc de Beaujolais' 'de champagne' and so forth an echo of the taste of the mother wine. The only German spirit which I have found worth commending is called *Enzian*; it has an aseptic taste of gentian. Mexico now increasingly exports tequila, the fiery spirit distilled from the century plant.

(i) GIN

THERE is little to be said of this most popular and most neutral of spirits. *London* gin has a strong scent – like a rather vulgar woman's perfume, to be truthful. It is either properly distilled and sufficiently matured, or it is not. Your tongue and the back of your throat will tell: reject what burns unpleasantly or has a metallic taste. Molasses is sometimes used for making gin; some gins, such as

Beefeater, are pure grain. *Plymouth* gin is similar but has rather more of the distinctive flat juniper taste. Coates' make it, from grain. 'Pink', that is with Angostura bitters, it is the favourite drink of the officers of the Royal Navy, as rum is of the ratings. It is half-way to *Hollands*, the original 'geneva' which has the juniper taste very markedly. This is much liked by many people, especially those who don't like London gin. It should be drunk before or after food; it is apt to be indigestible with food; it should be taken cold. All good Hollands still comes from Holland. Favourite brands are a matter of opinion; mine is Henkes' Oude, and next to it Bols.

(ii) RUMS

RUM is one of the best of spirits. It is the drink of pirates and sailors; it is as full of character as gin is without it. Its vendors, in general, do not appreciate it. They press on their customers recipes for cocktails, as if the best thing to do with it was to overwhelm its taste with orange juice and ice. They stress its warming and jovial character, as if its chief virtue was to make you rather uproarious. Yet rums are things of individuality; they differ among themselves as markedly as burgundies differ from clarets, and for similar reasons – difference of origin and varying methods of making.

Rum is made in Queensland, Mexico, India, Natal, and indeed anywhere where the sugar cane grows. But the France of the rum trade is the West Indies; only the West Indian rums are worth considering individually. There are no really old rums: rum merchants have never tried maturing rum as brandy is matured. Yet they may be mistaken: I have drunk some fifteen-year-old Jamaica, it was very much better than current rum and had acquired a remarkable smoothness and an odd bouquet, something like pineapple, but also something like amyl acetate, or whatever is the name of what women put on their fingernails. At the beginning of the First World War certain units of the British Expeditionary Force benefited by Admiralty or War Office over-buying ever since the Crimean war; they were served out fifty-year-old rum which astounded them. Suddenly (just after some of them had seen the Angels at Mons, it was commented) the nectar ran out, and they were back on the standard issue.

The Bordeaux of rum is Kingston, *Jamaica*. Jamaican rum is the best-known of all rums, and sets a standard for the rest. Jamaican laws are more stringent than others: any flavouring, except one drawn from the cane itself, is for example forbidden. There are three ways of classifying Jamaican (and other) rums. They can be classified by colour – dark or pale. However, darkness does not mean strength, as novelists think. It is caramel, a sharp (not sweet) decoction of the cane, which gives the colour, and also gives a bouquet. Incidentally, rum, despite its taste, contains no sugar. The sugar has already been extracted, and diabetics can safely drink all the rum that they can stand. Rums can also be classed as blended, or unblended; most rums are blended, and those that are not should be labelled as from such-and-such an 'Estate'. Rums can finally be classed according to their 'rummy' taste, and here the differences between the Islands are most individual. There are two extremes. In Jamaica the rum taste is purest and most clearly marked; in Cuba it is most lightly neutral. In between the other islands lie as it were at different points on a graph. Preferences among various brands must be personal: the names I shall mention are merely my own choice. Of Jamaican 'darks' I no longer can recommend Myers; its taste and bouquet have changed. Of lighter rums there is one which is notably clean in taste and guaranteed to leave no trace on the breath to rouse wifely reproaches: Appleton Estate (the yellow, not the white). *Trinidad* rums have a more aromatic and (to me) slightly orangey taste. Names: Caroni Estate, Fernandes, Siggert's Gold Label. The rum of *Barbados* has been described as 'like whisky'. The Mountgay liqueur rum from that island is my favourite of all rums. The *Dominica* rum is infrequent and not always too well distilled. Shillingford's has a curious raisiny flavour. The French island rums are coarse: only one, a *Martinique*, is worth prolonged attention. That is the St James' Plantations, which is carefully made from a delimited estate. All French rums tend to be dark, though there is some white Martinique. The *British Guiana* or *Demerara* rums frequently have a dry, quininey flavour, very useful to guard against oversweetness. One brand, Reflection, has a very favourable mark against it in my records; it is a Manzanilla among rums. The least rummy of all rums is Bacardi, which used to be made in Cuba and is now made in *Mexico*. It is used mostly in cocktails; it has almost lost its native character altogether.

(iii) BRANDY

THE best brandy in the world is *Cognac*. In a subject where almost any statement will be contradicted, that affirmation can be made with the knowledge that nobody will deny it unless he owns shares in some rival enterprise. The indifferent-to-wretched wine which is made around the town of Cognac in France has the unexplained property, when distilled, of producing a brandy with a taste and a series of scents unequalled anywhere. The area is delimited;

it lies within the two departments of Charente and Charente Maritime. (Until recently the latter was named Charente Inférieure, but nothing would persuade English and American buyers that this only meant Lower Charente; the name had to be changed by a special law.) It is divided into three large areas of Fins Bois, Bons Bois, Bois Ordinaires or Bois a Terroir, in descending order of quality. Round the town of Cognac itself are smaller areas, the Grande Champagne, the Petite Champagne and the Borderies, and from them come all the finest Cognacs. The name of 'Fine Champagne' is sometimes found on bottles; it means a mixture from the Champagnes. When any of those last four names is found on a label, the cognac should be excellent, but dear. But more usually cognac is bought upon the maker's name, to which is added a sign indicating its probable quality. Originally, there was a conventional system of stars – one star indicating a poor brandy fit only for cooking, or for drinking with soda water, three stars a good workaday brandy, five stars something highly refined. But stars are no certain guide now – the worst French brandy I ever drank had five stars round its cheating neck. If the firm is a good firm – say Hine or Martell – then its Three Star will be good and clean. But there are well-known firms (I have two at least in mind now) whose Three Star cannot be trusted. Dearer and also sweeter than the starred brandies are a whole series named V.S.O.P. ('very superior old pale'), and other more fanciful names. They are regarded as liqueur brandies; it is among them that are found most markedly the powerful perfume and flavour that distinguish cognacs. But you may find some that are glycerinely smooth, heavily syrupy, or taste strongly of vanilla; these are made for an ignorant market and should be avoided, unless you happen to like vanilla syrup. Anyway an after-dinner brandy is almost certain to be welcome if it comes out of a bottle labelled Hine, Otard, Delamain, Denis Mounié, Bisquit-Dubouché, or Exshaw, or is Martell's Cordon Argent or Extra, or an expensive Hennessey.

Cognacs which have a date are likely to be better than others. But the cult of ancient brandies is mostly nonsense. No spirit improves in bottle at all; the cobwebs and dust on the bottle the waiter shows you, even if they came there naturally, have no meaning. Nor does a brandy improve indefinitely in cask; it needs attention if it is not to develop an unpleasant taste. In particular, it needs 'refreshing' with a younger spirit. I have had from the same firm an '1885' and an '1873' of which the older was more fiery, less smooth, and in taste and probably in fact younger. It had just been 'refreshed'. This process has now been forbidden by the French government. The reform is well-meant, but it means that vintage brandies will shortly disappear, except for those which are refreshed outside France. In any case I should approach anything earlier than the twenties of the present century with deep caution; of 'Napoleon brandies', '1811 Cognacs', 'Year of the Comet', and so on, I would be completely sceptical.

The finer brandies are often drunk in balloon glasses. This is not necessary, for the standard tulip-shaped glass will not disperse the aroma, but balloons do bring out the bouquet more quickly and thoroughly. The cult of the balloon glass is carried to fantastic lengths: people will use glasses the size of a cheese-bell. Still, if you must go in for fantasies, it is more excusable with cognacs than anywhere else. The scent is powerful; you can get drunk on it alone. It is delightful; unlike the scent of a flower, it remains, and you can sniff it again and again. It is penetrating; if a cold is approaching, and your nose is closing up, sniff repeatedly a good liqueur brandy and the passages will be cleared. (This is not a permanent cure.)

The other main brandy area delimited in France is *Armagnac*, in the department of Gers, some way to the south of Bordeaux. It is divided into Haut-Armagnac, Tenareze and Bas-Armagnac. Armagnac brandies are less refined than cognacs, and their bouquet and taste have a more herbal quality. There is a recollection of sage, wild lavender, or perhaps thyme in them. Unlike cognac, which is improved by being slightly warmed, Armagnac is best drunk cool.

Outside France, brandies are made wherever wine is made, but only six of them deserve naming. The *Italian* and *German* can be good, so can the *Cyprus*. Keo is a brand name. *South Africa* makes a good dry liqueur brandy. Excellent brandy is made in *Australia*, but not often exported. Look, however, for the brand named St Agnes (three star or liqueur) and particularly Mildara Pot-still. Cape brandies and most Australians (not including St Agnes, which is nearer to a cognac) are to be classed with Armagnacs and treated similarly – that is, they may be drunk in balloons, but cool, not warmed. So treated, they are not just equal to the average Armagnac; the best brands are, in fact, superior. I have before now made the experiment of concealing the bottle names and offering them to experienced drinkers. My guests have rarely been able to pick out the Armagnac, and usually have preferred the Commonwealth brandies.

None of these however, in my experience, rise to the level of the best cognac, or have as yet claims to be 'great liqueur brandies'. There is only one country, *Spain*, which produces a highly distinctive brandy which can make such a claim. Spanish brandy has a strange 'smoky' taste in it; the taste can be acquired and gives great delight to those who have acquired it. 'Carlos I' is a good brand, so also is 'Fundador'.

(iv) WHISKY

APART from American whiskies – United States bourbon, Canadian rye, and variations on these – there are only two families of whisky worth writing about. The smaller, spelt 'whiskey', is the *Irish*. It is immediately distinguishable from Scotch by a smooth, slightly flat taste (comparable, at a distance, to Hollands). Its 'spread' is narrower than Scotch. It is never so good as a grand Glenlivet, but it is never so bad as a really vile public-house 'small Scotch' can be. (Not, at least, the legal brands of Irish: poteen can kill you.) The only brands which deserve mention are pot still whiskeys, not blended (except possibly the Ulster Bushmills) with patent still whiskey; only three matter: Jameson and Powers of Dublin and a Cork whiskey called Paddy. These three are all now owned by a combine called United Distillers of Ireland.

But *Scotch* is the whisky *par excellence*, imitated all over the world; and while elsewhere all the best of the Island's products are exported to earn hard currency, the Scots, as they have done for two hundred years, still keep their finest whisky for themselves. It is impossible to charge them successfully with selfishness in this. The rest of the world (they say) asks for blended whisky; do they not send abroad, even to England, whatever blends are asked for? If Lowlanders do not know that unblended whiskies have the most remarkable differences of taste and aroma, why trouble them with knowledge which would only increase their discontent with an already imperfect world? Morever, blending is a skilled craft, and in receiving a well-blended whisky the foreigner is being presented with something that may justly be described as a work of art.

Let him be grateful for that, and not seek to push his way into the artist's studio. Or if he must, let him take a ticket to the Highlands and travel – respectfully, man, at that.

The famous blended whiskies are a combination of malt whiskies made in pot stills, and grain whiskies made in patent stills. The pot stills are the traditional huge round kettles, with a great arm reaching out to carry the distilled alcohol into the cooling mechanism, which are pictured in old engravings. Patent stills look like two huge columns; they were invented by a man called Aeneas Coffey and they are enormously economical of labour and material. They produce a flood of characterless spirit; all the flavour and aroma in whisky comes from the old, expensive, capricious pot still. But in fairness it must be said that a diet of pure malt whiskies would strain the livers of any-body but a Highland trooper; for ordinary men the powerful nectar must be diluted with the more neutral spirit. The best blends will give you some information on their labels of the proportion of Highland malts, Lowland malts, or grains that they contain. If your wine merchant blends his own, as some still do, he will be pleased if you are intelligent enough to ask him for such information. Over half the whisky companies are controlled by one huge combine, which has till now sensibly allowed them to keep their separate character. One that is not is Bell's, whose Extra Special blend, and Blair Atholl unblended, are excellent.

The taste of the malts is distinctive, and is due to the factors of air, water, peat and barley. Air: it has been tried, but rarely with success, to distil good whisky near to a big city like Glasgow; the peculiar pure and soft air of the Highland hills is needed. Water: it may be possible che-mically to reproduce the burn waters used in the 'washing' process, but it has never been done yet; the substitutes leave a hard and tinny taste. Peat: fumes rise during the kiln drying which theoretically should not, but in fact do, affect the final product. Barley: local grown barley is no longer exclusively used, but it is carefully matched (and, at that, the older whisky-tasters claim that they can tell the difference when a barley 'just the same' has been brought in from abroad). Sherry casks, in which the whisky is matured, do have a distinct and rather 'fattening' effect on the taste, but their main use is to colour what is originally a white spirit. The shape of the still is most important; so is the skill of the stillman.

In Scotland, and rarely outside it, one may have the pleasure of tasting the unblended whiskies from which the blends are made. Nobody but a Glasgow spiv would put soda with these, or anything but perhaps a dash of water, which must be soft water, unchlorinated. Each has as marked a character as a claret; but the knowledge of them is not usually met with south of the Border. Their names are Gaelic music – Ardbeg, Talisker, Lagavulin, Balmenach, Glenlivet – and decade by decade they, too, are vanishing. They disappear into the vats of great companies offering 'Best Scotch'; Lagavulin itself, reputed by some the king of all whiskies, has almost vanished from the market.

On the west coast, in Argyll, was once a small group of heavy whiskies produced at Campbelltown; they are nearly all gone now. Perhaps they were a little too heavy, unblended, for a modern sedentary town dweller. But only a short way north, on the island of Islay, is a larger group of whiskies fit for all, including the royal Lagavulin and the scarcely inferior Ardbeg. Tobermory on Mull, commended in earlier editions of this book, is only a memory; but there is still on Skye Talisker, last survivor of a half-dozen distilleries. Round the tip end of Scotland in the far Orkneys, drink Highland Park; dropping south along the east coast to Brora, take Clynelish. Now, as you circle round the longest tongue of the Moray Firth, you are approaching the most famous glen in the world – Glenlivet. Only one whisky, Smith's, has the right to call itself 'Glenlivet' alone, *tout court*, as only one white burgundy has the right to call itself Le Montrachet. George Smith, in 1824, secured that right, by licence of the Duke of Gordon, by two hair-trigger pistols and by the aid of four of the toughest servants he could recruit. But there are a score of other distilleries on Spey side, or at least not far from the Glen, which are entitled to add the great name to their own. So, as a very honest burgundy calls itself Puligny-Montrachet, there are fine whiskies calling themselves Glenlossie-Glenlivet, Dufftown-Glenlivet, Glengrant-Glenlivet, and so on, of which the last-named requires a special mention for its dryness and individual flavour.

Good luck, or a Highland friend, or an unusual wine merchant may enable you to taste one of these or twenty others; if so, it will be an experience which even a wine-lover can envy.

(v) LIQUEURS

THE publicity for the better established liqueurs is impressive. The dearest, Chartreuse, for example, claims to be made from 130 herbs according to a secret formula for the 'elixir of long life' given to the Carthusian monks in 1605 by the Marshal d'Estrées. It may be so; and herbs do have some medicinal properties. But it is extremely doubtful if in liqueur form they have any health giving effects. A possible exception could be Raspail, which was thought out painstakingly by an eminent and very honourable doctor of the last century. I think he was deluded, all the same. Nor do they mature with age. Nigel Dugdale, once proprietor of an excellent London restaurant, used to sell an admirably smooth 'Liqueur des Anciens Moines'; he told me he made it himself every quarter-day in the cellar. Liqueurs are manufactured drinks from the equivalent of a kitchen. If the recipe and the cook are good, they are good. If they are distilled from a mixture of alcohol and herbs, fruits, seeds, barks or whatever it may be, they are likely to be better than plain alcohol into which sugar and a flavouring has been poured. But either way they are not naturally developed drinks, and all that I can usefully do is to list a score of better known specimens according to flavour and origin:

Name	Flavour	Origin
Advocaat	Custard and brandy	Holland
Anis	Aniseed	France, Spain
Apricot brandy (Barak)	Apricots	Hungary, Holland
Benedictine	Herbal	France
Cassis	Blackcurrant	France
Chartreuse	Mixed herbs	France
Cherry brandy	Cherry	Denmark, Britain, Holland
Cloc	Herbs and orange	Denmark
Cointreau	Tangerine peel	France
Cordial Médoc	Claret	France
Crème de Menthe	Mint	France
Curaçao	Orange	Holland
Drambuie	Honey and Whisky	Scotland

Name	*Flavour*	*Origin*
Goldwasser	Has gold specks	Germany
Grand Marnier	Orange peel	France
Izarra	Wild herbs	France
Kümmel	Caraway seed	Holland and elsewhere
Maraschino	Nuts, cherry stones	Yugoslavia
Marnique	Quince	Australia
Peach brandy	Peaches	Hungary
Raspail	Doctor's herbs	France
Sloe gin	Sloes	Britain
Strega	Veal stuffing	Italy
Van der Hum	Tangerines	Cape
Vieille Cure	Sage stuffing	France

149